A History of SOUTHAMPTON
In Picture Postcards

Clive Brooks with Peter Boyd-Smith

Ensign
PUBLICATIONS

First published in 1989 by Ensign Publications

British Library Cataloguing in Publication Data
Brooks, Clive
    A history of Southampton in picture postcards.
    1. Hampshire. Southampton, 1837–
    I. Title
    942.2' 76081

    ISBN 1 85455 031 4

Ensign Publications
2 Redcar St
Shirley
Southampton SO1 5LL

Edited by David Graves.

Typeset by CAS Limited, Southampton.
Designed by Mark Eslick.
Printed in the E.E.C.

Contents

Foreword ———————————————————— 4

CHAPTER ONE   Horse Trams and Beyond ———————— 9

CHAPTER TWO   Southampton, Ships and the Sea ———— 24

CHAPTER THREE   The Villages of Southampton ————— 39

CHAPTER FOUR   The War Years ——————————— 49

CHAPTER FIVE   The Centre of Southampton ————— 60

CHAPTER SIX   Bridges, Floating and Otherwise ——— 79

CHAPTER SEVEN   Advertisements, Announcements, Trade Cards
and Assorted, Printed Ephemera ————— 84

Bibliography ————————————— 88

Dedications

To Peryl, Kit, Jim & Tony with all best wishes
Clive Brooks

For Anna, Simon, Paul, Mark, Martin and Roy, this is what your City used to look like
Peter Boyd-Smith

FOREWORD

Monorails and marinas, skyscrapers and shopping malls — Southampton is once again in the first division of commercial enterprise. Considerably aided by an efficient network of motorways and with its commanding position at the centre of the country's most convenient maritime gateway, Southampton is well equipped to face the challenges of the next century in much the same way as it met the challenges of the late 19th century.

Much of the charm and character of Southampton before the Second World War disappeared in the Blitz, since then the developers have 'urbanised' the remainder. Some call it progress, others like myself, call it a shame, question the requirement for such radical change and mourn the passing of a quieter, bygone age.

The remnants of earlier ages of expansion have provided the impetus for a good part of the more recent developments. Ocean Village for instance, a mixed retail and leisure facility, has given a new purpose to part of the extensive and now largely redundant, older dock areas.

In addition to the Ocean Dock, there is the Town, Empress and Princess Alexandra basins each with their own quay–side property, now much sought after by land–hungry developers. With the happy precedence of Ocean Village, Shamrock Quay at Millbank and now Town Quay, it bodes well for the future of the area that at last originality of thought, city planners and commercial gain seem to be able to walk side by side.

We can never bring the old Southampton back; however thanks to the efforts of local collectors, most notably in this selection my colleague Peter Boyd-Smith of Cobwebs Memorabilia, we can do the very next best thing and recall those long lost distant times in vivid detail, with words and old pictures.

Throughout the compilation of this publication, we have endeavoured through careful choice, to evoke myriad memories — some happy, some sad, but all fond — of our City. I do hope that we have succeeded and that you enjoy this armchair journey in time. My most cordial thanks are offered to the large number of people who have willingly placed useful information within my grasp, especially Stuart Links, Mick Hillier and Brian Ticehurst by whose valuable help, the present result has been obtained.

Clive Brooks
September 1989.
Southampton

Introduction

Our story begins in 1860, when the advent of steam propulsion at sea had already made Southampton an attractive base for the fledgling steamship companies. It was steam power on land that provided the town with its first, useful links with London and later served to complete its supremacy as the principal Empire sea port.

By the late 1880's there was a considerable passenger trade through the port, and the problem of providing further dock accommodation became paramount. With ships getting bigger, the financially stretched Dock Company found it very difficult to develop the facilities in line with the growing requirements, this had already resulted in P & O deserting the port. Plans were subsequently made for a new 16 acre dock with 3,300 feet of quay which was to cost £200,000. The Southampton Corporation duly prepared a Parliamentary Bill to raise the money so that it could, in turn, be lent to the Dock Company. The capital proved difficult to raise, and the scheme looked set to fall through until it was rescued at the last minute by the London & South Western Railway who stepped in to provide a loan of £250,000. This led to the opening, on the 26th of July 1890, of the Empress Dock by Queen Victoria. Two years later, the Dock Company, unable to develop further, agreed to an offer of purchase by the L&SWR. The new owners made a bold statement; they would turn Southampton into the "Liverpool of the South". This confidence proved well founded, by 1912, Southampton had become the main, North Atlantic passenger port of Great Britain.

The swing to the south had begun three years after the Empress Dock opened, when the American Line transferred its New York service down from Liverpool. Further momentum came when, in 1907, White Star's North Atlantic Express Service followed suit, with the *Adriatic*, the largest vessel in the world at that time, arriving at the port on May the 29th. In response to this, a further 15½ acre deep water dock was constructed and opened in 1911, originally named the White Star Dock, later known simply as the Ocean Dock. It was from here that the ill–fated *Titanic* sailed on 10th April 1912. Some 600 Southampton families would be affected by her tragic loss.

It soon became obvious that the passage of emigrants from Southampton could provide another source of trade. The Southampton Emigration Society was formed and embarked on a campaign to persuade the Colonial Secretary to recognise Southampton as an emigrant depot. This was successful, and after a visit by the commissioners, emigrant ships began leaving for Australia. Such traffic tested Southampton's suitability as a port for embarkation and disembarkation of large numbers of passengers, and it was not long before the facilities were tested in more pressing circumstances.

During two years of the Crimean War, over 100,000 men and 20,000 horses were transported. However, as the 1850's closed, it became clear that it would not be enough just to bring the troops home — the carnage meant that there would have to be medical facilities for them on their return. Consequently a site was chosen for a new military hospital at Netley, to be named Royal Victoria, in honour of the Queen, who laid the foundation stone on the 19th May 1856. The hospital has now long been demolished with just the old chapel remaining.

Several shipbuilding yards rose to prominence in the area, and along with them, keen to share in the prosperity, were the smaller boat and yacht builders. One of the principal small yards was that of Alfred Payne and Dan Hatcher, who specialized in the production of the Itchen Ferry Boat. Other notable yards were Arrow and Fay's which came together after 1912 to form Camper and Nicholson.

Northam Iron Works launched its first iron steamer, *Pride of the Waters*, onto the Itchen in October 1840. Their big opportunity came with the construction of mail ships for the large shipping companies who were now operating from the new docks. At the time, the Northam Works were in an enviable position, being the only such establishment on the river until the Woolston Yard was developed in 1876.

Due to the new dock facilities, there became considerable opportunities in Southampton for employment in shipbuilding and repairing, even before the docks had been expanded. One of the most important of these was the Oswald Mordaunt yard at Woolston, which between 1879 and 1889, launched over 100 ships. When the yard closed it was near disaster for the population of Woolston, as most of its men were employed at the works. To ease the situation, a consortium was formed to maintain shipbuilding on the site and this led to the founding of the Southampton Naval Works. However, only eighteen ships were built there before this was also forced into liquidation. Shipbuilding had again proved a tenuous occupation for the working men of Woolston.

This situation remained until Fay's the yacht builders attempted a rejuvenation of the yard. By 1899, they were negotiating with a firm called Morden Carney who took over the yard for a short time, until, in 1904, the firm of John. I. Thornycroft, keen to expand from a cramped yard on the Thames at Chiswick, took over the yard which they have continued to use to the present day.

The Borough was fast expanding, by the turn of the century, the population already numbered some 105,000. This unfortunately meant that many of the elegant parks were sold for building purposes. Disease reared its ugly head in overcrowded, slum areas of the town — a cholera epidemic in 1848–9 claimed hundreds of lives, and considerable alarm was caused when another epidemic struck in 1865 killing 41 people. Even with such serious outbreaks on their hands, the Board of Health had an uphill struggle trying to convince the Corporation of the need for action. It was due to their perseverance however that, in 1875, a scheme for draining Portswood was finally approved. However, in the lower part of Southampton drainage remained a problem, and it wasn't until a particularly nasty flood occurred that a scheme for sewers was provided for this part of town.

Southampton did have a number of fine facilities, even its own racecourse! This was originally laid out in 1822, and revived in 1860 by the Mayor, Frederick Perkins. The first race meetings were well attended by the rich and titled, but within a few years they had been chased away by a rowdy element of drunken racegoers who took over the meetings, this eventually led to the programme being scrapped altogether in 1881.

New schools and churches were provided during this period, some of the larger private houses were converted into educational establishments. The teaching of the poor was provided for by National or Church Schools, twelve of which were established in 1858. But it was the £42,000 that the Corporation inherited from the eccentric recluse Henry Hartley, that led to the formation of the Hartley Institute in the High Street. This became, in the 1890's, the Hartley College, then in 1902, the Hartley University College, and Southampton University College in 1914. It was moved to a new site at Highfield to become the University of Southampton in 1952.

By the end of the century, the suburbs of Southampton were well served by railway stations; at Swaythling, St Deny's, Bitterne, Woolston, Millbrook and Northam. These were originally supplemented by horse omnibus services. However as early as the 1870's, the horse omnibus service had already begun to prove inadequate for the growing needs of the population. It was replaced in 1879 by the first horse drawn trams — so popular were these that over 3,000 passengers used them on their first day alone — which meant takings of £25! The main depot was at Portswood with stabling for 100 horses, with room for 60 more at a Shirley depot. In addition, there were 35 in a shed at Highfield and a dozen more behind the Bitterne Park Hotel.

Expansion of the town continued, and the new century brought new housing in St Deny's, Bevois Valley, Newtown, Northam and Nichol's Town as well as in western areas such as Freemantle and Shirley. Across the Itchen at Woolston the population had grown to some 10,000 people. Bitterne too, was also beginning to develop.

To assist traffic flow, and because of competition from Cobden Bridge, the Northam Bridge Company replaced its wooden structure with one of iron in 1889. Another key event in the town's development was the purchase by the Southampton Corporation of the Electric Light and Power Company which had established a generating station at Back-of-the-Walls. By March 1899, the first electric street lights were in operation in the town. At the time, there was little call for electricity during the day, and so, with the surplus of generated power, the decision was made to electrify the tramways, with the first route to Shirley being inaugurated on 22nd January 1900.

As with any large urban population of this period, slum areas began to emerge. In Southampton, these were especially prevalent in the older parts of the city; one local politician wrote:

> "There are small, close, dirty and evil smelling streets generally blocked up at one end and sometimes at both. . . a maze of little courts and passages with wretched tumbledown houses closely packed with human beings with no provision for decency or cleanliness and the tribes of children, hungry, dirty, barefooted and wild. . ."

In a bid to ease the problem, the tactfully named Housing of the Working Classes Act was passed in 1890 and a scheme prepared for the redevelopment of the worst area — the slums between Blue Anchor Lane, Simnel Street and Castle Lane where the population density was 441 per acre, in contrast to 14.5 in the genteel environs of Portswood.

Meanwhile, a new pier was constructed on 4½ acres of tidal foreshore. When it was opened at a cost of about £40,000 by the Duke of Connaught in 1892, it was the largest steamer and pleasure pier on the south coast. A bandstand was originally provided, but this was subsequently converted into a large pavilion. Ten steamer berths were built, and competition for excursions began to increase between Red Funnel and Bristol Channel operators P & A Cambell, who brought their steamer *Cambria* to Southampton.

It wasn't only ships that Southampton was ideally placed to construct and maintain. Another transport industry sprang up in 1913 — the construction of seaplanes and flying boats. The area was ideal because of the availability of boat-building skills combined with sheltered waters for testing, and the proximity of the new Naval Air Station at nearby Calshot Castle. In fact, the seed of Southampton's aviation history had been planted three years earlier in 1910, when the Hampshire Aero Club was formed. The first factory for the construction of flying boats was established on the Woolston shore of the Itchen in 1913 by Noel Pemberton Billing, under the management of Hubert Scott-Paine. The machines that emerged from the shed were called *Supermarines* — the name eventually given to this legendary company.

Before aviation could become firmly established, war was declared on 4th August 1914, and Southampton became the principal port of embarkation for the British Expeditionary Force. The port's trooping facilities were once again put to the test, this time with much more confidence, as, since the Crimean War, there had been the South African conflict of 1899–1902, when over half a million men together with 27,922 horses had passed through the docks.

As the Great War became a harsh reality, large sections of the Common were taken over by the military, with much of the area covered with tents and huts. From the Common, columns of troops marched down the tree-lined Avenue to the docks, singing to the accompaniment of military bands. Inevitably, Southampton once again became the major return port for the wounded, and a number of schools and country houses in the area were hastily converted into makeshift hospitals. In addition, the capacity of the military hospital at Netley, where many of the worst casualties were treated, was doubled, many of the wounded being housed in temporary buildings constructed in the grounds.

During the conflict, the total number of British, Colonial and American men who passed through the port totalled 8,149,685 — a daily average exceeding 4,000. A Cenotaph was unveiled on November 6th 1920 to commemorate 2,008 of the town's own dead. Its design became the prototype for the National Cenotaph which stands in Whitehall and figures annually as the centrepiece of our Remembrance Sunday parade.

When war was declared, Thornycrofts started converting passenger ships into troop transports, and within a few days the yard had also obtained orders for four destroyers. Throughout the war, many new warships were built at Woolston, making it the third largest supplier of destroyers to the Navy.

In September 1914, Pemberton Billing made over his factory to his manager Hubert Scott-Paine, who managed to secure sufficient work building aircraft designed by other firms, and repairing battle damaged aircraft, to secure his future and register the firm. By 1916, it had been renamed the Supermarine Aviation Works; the team included a young man called R.J. Mitchell — later to design the *Spitfire*. The flying boats that Scott-Paine had built during the war to Air Department specifications were converted, after the conflict, into the first civilian, passenger-carrying craft. Supermarine themselves inaugurated a new flying boat service on 16th August 1919, the original intention being to provide a local service to Bournemouth and the Isle of Wight. However, a cross-channel ferry strike just after the service was inaugurated, enabled Supermarine to move in with a flying boat service to both Cherbourg and Le Havre.

Consequently, Woolston became the first marine airport in the country, and by 1923, regular flying boat services were underway using three Supermarine *Sea Eagle* flying boats designed by R.J. Mitchell. In March of 1924, Imperial Airways was formed from the leading civil airlines of that time, which led to a large number of new planes being ordered. These were Armstrong Whitworth *Ensign* monoplanes with 123 foot wingspans, which were built on the Hamble. The famous *Empire* flying boats of 18 tons, also made their first appearance, with the operation eventually being based at Hythe.

Southampton's airport at Eastleigh, bought by the Corporation in 1932, had, by 1934, become the country's third busiest terminal — Croydon was first, with Portsmouth a close second.

The two decades between the World Wars were undoubtedly Southampton's golden era, with great prosperity coming from the enormous passenger liners that used the port. The London & South Western Railway were pleased to welcome Cunard to Southampton after the war when they decided to follow White Star's lead and transfer their operation to the port. The *Mauretania* inaugurated their association when she sailed from Southampton for the first time on the 6th March 1920. Extra repair facilities were required, and this led to the construction of a floating dock capable of taking liners of upto 60,000 tons. The berthing facilities were also extended once more, this time utilising the mouth of the River Test, where further mudflats were reclaimed and the Western Docks constructed.

By the 1930's, the floating dock was proving inadequate for the increased tonnages using the port, and hence a new graving dock was built. It was opened by King George V and Queen Mary on the 26th of July 1933. This could take vessels up to 100,000 tons, and had been designed with Cunard's *Queen Mary* very much in mind. At 1200 feet × 135 feet and with a depth of 45 feet, it was the largest graving dock ever built, and cost an estimated £1.8 million. By 1933, Southampton was already handling over

75,000 cruise passengers, and that only made up one seventh of the entire passenger traffic.

New offices for the Harbour Board were built at Town Quay and opened on 8th September 1925. The office had a domed roof with a circular hall decorated with bas–relief panels from the White Star liner *Teutonic*. Soon the distinctive dome had competition, a similar one was given to the Royal Pier building a few hundred yards away. The pier was immensely popular; during the bank holiday of August 1936, 13,700 people visited it, and a further 27,000 passengers were carried by Red Funnel Steamers for pleasure cruises and general packet journeys.

Another notable construction during this period was Southampton's new Civic Centre. The foundation stone was laid by Albert, Duke of York, on the 1st July 1930, and the offices opened two years later on the 8th November 1932.

Unprecedented commercial growth meant that there was a severe shortage of housing in the Borough, and a Council building programme was now deemed necessary. The first site purchased for such development was Hampton Park, where, between 1921 and 1924, some 382 houses were built. Other estates of this period included the Freshfield Estate at Freemantle and a scheme in Woolston which included Spring Road, Spring Close and Knighton Road, built using direct labour. The largest estate was at Burgess Road between Bassett and Swaythling, and this included the well–known "flower roads" such as Pansy and Violet etc. The completed Burgess Road development totalled 1,164 houses, costing £467,984-0s-3d! During 1928, the Housing Committee began investigating new site possibilities, the first being at Merry Oak, and by June 1929 some 334 houses had been built — and so it went on.

All this made even greater demands on public transport, and although motor buses had been introduced in 1900, it was not until the first war that they were deemed reliable enough to operate on routes not also served by trams. Hard on the heels of this came the advent of the private motor car, which was becoming more affordable. In December 1935, Wadham Brothers opened an art deco style garage in Banister Road, and by 1939 there were 132 petrol stations within Southampton. Then just as Southampton's future looked assured, the Second World War came along to darken the new optimism of the late 30's. It caused terrible destruction and indeed death on an unprecedented scale, Southampton would never be the same again.

During the dark days of the late 30's, there took place an event in the town which was truly instrumental in the country's victory over the Nazis — the test flight of the new Supermarine *Spitfire* aircraft at Eastleigh Airport by test pilot Mutt Summers. Three months later Supermarine was to receive its first order for 310 of the new fighters. Sadly R.J. Mitchell, who had been terminally ill for some time, died on the 11th June 1937, before he saw his greatest design fly in anger.

War was declared in September 1939, and over 14,000 children were evacuated to the comparative safety of the countryside many to return not too many months later. The first bombs fell early on the morning of 20th June 1940 in a series of small daylight raids which were mere tasters for the blitz of the town in November and December. On 11th September the Cunliffe-Owen aircraft factory, which had opened just before the War, received a direct hit, and Supermarine was bombed on the 24th and 26th September. Aircraft production continued by the simple expedient of dispersing the construction of the *Spitfire* across the whole of the south of England, and by placing specialised work in the hands of sub–contractors.

It was on the 23rd of November 1940 that the first sustained night attack took place and the real blitz began. Just after 6.30pm a large number of incendiaries fell on the eastern side of the city, followed by three hours of relentless bombardment when nearly 4000 incendiaries and 860 high explosive bombs rained down. The next attack came the following Saturday night, the 30th of November, with the siren sounding at 6.25pm, and bombardment continuing until 3.00am the next morning. It started yet again that evening causing death and devastation on a hitherto unheard of scale. It wasn't until 8.00pm on 5th November 1944 — ironically enough bonfire night — that the final "raider passed" signal was given.

During the early summer of 1944, Southampton became a series of vast linear camps with the approaches to what was left of the town packed with columns of vehicles all converging upon the docks. On Monday 5th June 1944, the order was given and the vast armada finally sailed. The departure of the invasion force was, and remains one of the largest dock handling operations ever seen, between D-Day and the end of the War, 2.5 million tons of stores, 257,680 vehicles, 21,000 railway wagons, 770 locomotives, 39 ambulance trains, and 16 mobile workshops left the docks together with 3.5 million troops.

On Tuesday 8th May 1945, the day set aside for the formal declaration of peace, there were 20,000 people gathered outside the Civic Centre to hear the relaying of the Prime Minister's speech. This was followed by a service of thanksgiving, where attention was drawn to the important task of rebuilding the shattered city. The maritime heart of Southampton returned when the *Queen Elizabeth* and *Queen Mary* sailed back into port after their wartime absence. After both liners had been extensively refitted, they entered passenger service again in 1946 and 1947 respectively.

The most pressing social problem at the end of the War was that of housing, replacing the 4,278 properties that had been destroyed. As the inhabitants began to return, the pressure on accommodation became intense, and so hundreds of pre–fabricated bungalows were erected. The first of these "prefab" areas was in Dale Valley Road, Itchen, it was completed by November 1945 utilising prisoner–of–war labour. The first contract for brick–built housing was for 100 homes at Weston Park, with the first of these handed over on the 16th October 1946. By April 1948, the 2000th post–war house had been completed.

The mainspring of the Corporation's housing policy was the building of the Millbrook Housing Estate of 3,217 dwellings, followed by those at Harefield, Thornhill and, in the 1960's, at Townhill Park. High rise developments were very much in vogue at this time and on the western edge of the City (status was granted by Royal Charter in 1964) the fifteen storey Redbridge Tower was constructed; the 25 storey Millbrook Tower, last of its breed, was "topped off" in 1965.

Meanwhile, the aviation business had continued to expand, and BOAC was formed out of Imperial Airways. Grand plans were made to re-establish flying boat services, but by 1949 most routes were already becoming unprofitable as land—based aircraft began to take over. This led to the closing down, in 1951, of the Hythe base, with Aquila, the holiday airline as the last local operator; they eventually gave up the base in 1958.

With more jet airliners crossing the Atlantic, there were less passengers for the great liners. Most people now preferred the newer novelty of flying quickly over the waves rather than a few leisurely days spent ploughing through them. Consequently, the fortunes of the steamship companies using the port waned, and before it was really grasped another great era had passed.

The *QE2* and *Canberra* carried on the tradition and are justly claimed as Southampton ships. However, while Southampton's air and sea traffic was on the decline, road traffic was on the increase, necessitating a new bridge over the River Test and a gradual widening of the main coastal road into a dual carriage—way with flyovers at Redbridge and Millbrook. There was however one natural barrier left to conquer — the River Itchen at Woolston.

For many years, the floating bridges had been overcrowded, many motorists hated the long wait at either end. A bridge here had been originally planned as far back as 1920, the proposal was revived unsuccessfully in 1947. It was deferred in view of the work needed at Northam Bridge which was replaced by a concrete structure in 1954. A Bill for the Itchen bridge was prepared for Parliament in 1960. It would have a central span of not less than 350 feet and a clearance of 80 feet at high water to allow the passage of ships on the river. The scheme looked set to go ahead until the Ministry of Transport decided that it was unnecessary and refused to provide three quarters of the capital cost that they were being asked for. They argued that their south coast trunk road, later to become the M27, provided the necessary access.

Consequently, it wasn't until 1970 that the Council decided to press ahead with a bridge as a local scheme financed out of local funds, much of which would be recouped in tolls. The Council finally agreed to a tender of £5,710,630 in February 1974, and the bridge was opened on Wednesday 1st June 1977. Ten days later, on Saturday 11th June, the floating bridge ceased operation and another chapter in Southampton's long and illustrious past was at an end.

SOUTHAMPTON & ITCHEN FLOATING BRIDGE

NOTICE.

On WEDNESDAY, August 15th, 1860, at the Guildhall, Southampton,

TOM COLE,

A Plasterer, employed on the Netley Hospital Works, appeared before the County Magistrates to answer a complaint for having refused to pay the Company the Double Toll chargeable after Bridge hours. He was ordered to pay the amount claimed and 7s. 6d. costs.

The Company have instructed their Collectors or Boatmen to demand payment of the legal Toll in all cases, and have determined to protect the men in their employ in the discharge of their duties from assault, and will take steps in all cases to prevent evasion of the Tolls.

BY ORDER,

JAS. C. SHARP,
CLERK.

August 17, 1860.

FORBES AND BENNETT, PRINTERS, SOUTHAMPTON.

Southampton and Itchen Floating Bridge Company.

INCREASED ACCOMMODATION.

NOTICE TO THE PUBLIC.

In consequence of the Steam Launch being now on the passage, the Directors are enabled to give Increased Facilities for Crossing the River:

On and after MONDAY, July 15th, 1878, the Bridge will make a passage from each side of the River—

Every Quarter-of-an-hour,

Instead of every Twenty Minutes as heretofore, making

Eight Trips Every Hour,

Instead of Six Trips, as hitherto.

The Bridge will Run as follows:

FROM SOUTHAMPTON.	FROM WOOLSTON.
At the Hour	At 7½ Minutes past the Hour
At Quarter-past the Hour	At 22½ Minutes past the Hour
At Half-past the Hour	At 37½ Minutes past the Hour
At Quarter to the Hour	At 52½ Minutes past the Hour

The STEAM LAUNCH "WOOLSTON"

Will also make 8 Trips every hour and will run as follows:

FROM SOUTHAMPTON.	FROM WOOLSTON.
When the Bridge leaves Woolston	When the Bridge leaves Southampton

To ensure success and punctuality in these arrangements, Carriages should be at the side of departure three minutes, and Foot Passengers two minutes, before the times above-named.

BY ORDER OF THE BOARD,

WM. GODDARD LANKESTER,
MANAGER.

SOUTHAMPTON: "HAMPSHIRE INDEPENDENT" OFFICE, PRINTED BY A. DYER.

Five Pounds
REWARD.

Southampton & Itchen Floating Bridge & Roads
COMPANY.

Whereas, some evil disposed person or persons did on Sunday night, the 20th inst., take from her moorings one of the Ferry Boats belonging to the Company and then left her to drift with the tide, being afterwards picked up in Dibden Bay.

And Whereas the offence of casting off the Company's Boats has been before repeatedly committed, the Company will give the above reward for such information as will lead to a conviction of the Offender or Offenders.

By Order,

JAS. C. SHARP,
CLERK TO THE COMPANY.

Southampton, November, 22, 1860.

FORBES & BENNETT, PRINTERS, SOUTHAMPTON.

CHAPTER ONE

Horse trams and beyond

TOP LEFT: The connection between Southampton and its suburbs was originally met by railway links and horse omnibus services. The latter ran between Terminus Station and both Portswood and Shirley. However, the horse omnibus system soon proved to be inadequate for the growing needs of the population, and, in 1872, the Corporation were approached by the British and Foreign Tramway Company. Their scheme was rejected because it was thought that it didn't have the community's best interests at heart, and four years later, Southampton Tramways Company was formed.

ABOVE: Work began on laying tram tracks for horse drawn vehicles in the summer of 1878. On Saturday 3rd May 1879, the Government Inspector, Major General Hutchinson, gave his approval to the lines, and services began on the following Monday. This photograph shows one of the twin–decked trams in the High Street, Below Bar.

BOTTOM LEFT: The inauguration of the first electric tram service to run between Stag Gates and Holy Rood on the 15th of May 1900. Alderman Dunsford, Chairman of the Tramways Committee prepares to drive away.

SOUTHAMPTON CORPORATION TRAMWAYS.

NOTICE !!

SHIRLEY SECTION

Reconstruction of the Permanent Way for Electric Traction.

On and after WEDNESDAY NEXT, JULY 12th, 1899 until further notice) the Shirley Cars to and from Town and Portswood will run to

KINGSTON ROAD ONLY

Busses will run to and from Kingston Road and Shirley.

A Transfer Service cannot there be guaranteed, but every effort will be made to meet the public convenience.

GEORGE T. CARNON, Manager.
Managerial Offices, July 3rd, 1899.

BY ORDER.

Southampton Car Passing Through the Bargate

Once upon a time wicked people were beheaded at the Bargate......

MIND YOUR HEADS!!!

To-day even good-law-abiding citizens find their heads in jeopardy there......

TOP LEFT: The Portswood Hotel in 1892. These are staff from the Portswood horse tram depot, next door. There were over 100 horses at this depot, with another 60 at the Shirley depot, 35 more stabled at Highfield and 12 more behind the Bitterne Park Hotel.

ABOVE: This photograph was taken in 1900 at the newly–formed Southampton Corporation Tramway's shed in Portswood. It shows some of the new fleet of electric tramcars that had recently become familiar sights on the city's streets.

BOTTOM LEFT: The Bargate had, for many years, been a difficult obstacle for traffic. As far back as January 1899, the Corporation discussed the question of building roads around it. There was even talk about increasing the central carriageway by doing away with the original arch in favour of a modern one. Discussions went as far as to consider the sale of the complete monument to the Americans! In the event, P.J. Baker, the General Manager of the tramways, introduced an enclosed tram using a low–wheeled truck, with a distinctive roof, moulded to the contours of the arch. To ensure necessary clearance, the roadway under the arch was lowered and, apparently, there was some secret, late–night hammering and chiselling that removed the inner moulding at the centre of the arch — mud was carefully applied to this afterwards to disguise the work.

TOP LEFT: Two trams clatter past the drinking fountain on the approach to the floating bridge. This scene was saved for posterity on 18th April 1949.

ABOVE: Forty—nine years after they had first run, the era of the electric tram in Southampton was at an end. The services were soon to be replaced by motor buses, passenger transport had come full circle. This photograph was taken on 13th June 1948 in the Portswood depot.

BOTTOM LEFT: A football special! This tram was pressed into service to carry supporters to a Saints versus Birmingham match, at the Dell on 13th June 1948, this photograph was taken on the Esplanade route opposite the Royal Pier.

"WARNING"
BARGATE ARCH
Passengers must be seated whilst the car is passing under BARGATE
AND MUST NOT TOUCH THE WIRE

TOP LEFT: The last tram to run in Southampton. This photograph was taken on 31st December 1949. The trams had been a feature of Southampton for almost fifty years, and were replaced with *Guy Arab* diesel buses.

ABOVE: Many of the old tramcars were sent to a scrapyard at St Deny's. Some of the bodies were sold off for £10 each, and found new uses as garden sheds and chicken houses in the area. A few of the closed top vehicles went into service in Leeds, but the others were left to rot in the graveyard, a sad reminder of the end of an era.

BOTTOM LEFT: A bus load of Southampton residents take to the roads on August 14th 1921 for a summer outing to Gough's Caves at Cheddar, where this photograph was taken. Convertible charabancs such as this were common at the time.

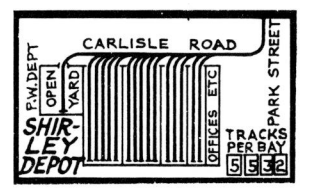

14

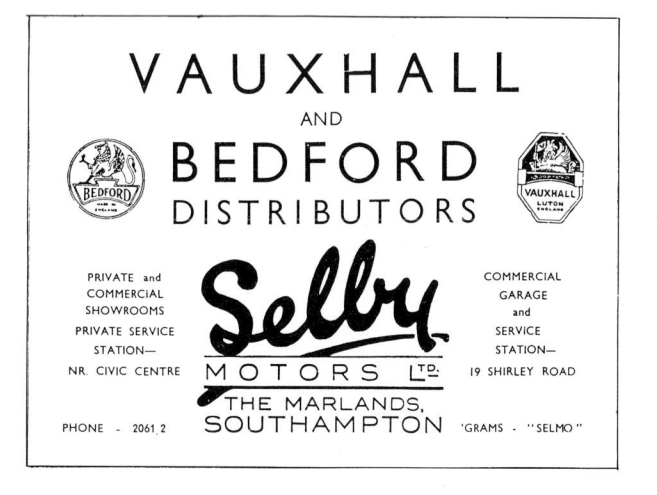

TOP LEFT: Another outing, this time on board one of Royal Blue's charabancs.

ABOVE: In this photograph, a *Guy Arab* diesel bus found itself in the ditch en route from Southampton to Blackfield near Hythe, this was a vehicle owned by Hants and Dorset.

BOTTOM LEFT: An eager group of youngsters have helped this unfortunate delivery-man to salvage his cargo of bread. This local scene would be repeated many times as the roads started to get congested with private and commercial vehicles.

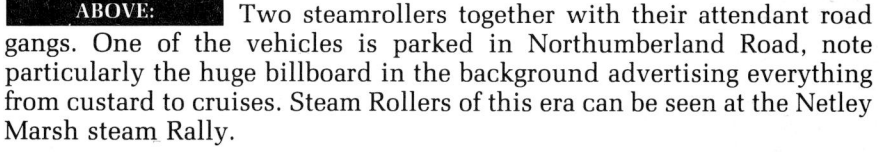

ABOVE: Two steamrollers together with their attendant road gangs. One of the vehicles is parked in Northumberland Road, note particularly the huge billboard in the background advertising everything from custard to cruises. Steam Rollers of this era can be seen at the Netley Marsh steam Rally.

BOTTOM LEFT: Situated next to what is now South Western House, this is the frontage of the original Docks Station. For a number of years it lay empty. Now, in line with much of the surrounding area, it has been 'developed' and has become a nightclub and casino.

L. S. W. R. Southampton Express

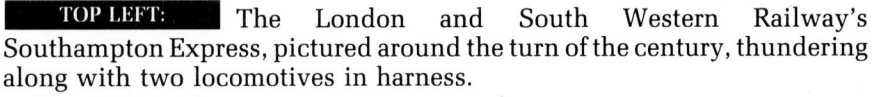

TOP LEFT: The London and South Western Railway's Southampton Express, pictured around the turn of the century, thundering along with two locomotives in harness.

ABOVE: Railways of course provided the link between the Ocean Terminal and the rest of the rail network. There were many such trains, each with names relating to the line they were serving. These included the *Cunarder*, and, in this photograph, the *Holland American*.

BOTTOM LEFT: A closer view of the *Queen Elizabeth* alongside the Ocean Terminal. The *Queens* always insisted on having the very best British provisions for their passengers, and were keen to provide every home comfort — even traditional marmalade on the breakfast table.

ABOVE: The new electric tram service to Shirley was inaugurated on the 22nd January 1900, using surplus electricity from the Back-of-the-Walls generating station, originally installed to provide street lighting. This view shows Above Bar and the newly arrived Plummer Roddis store on the corner of Commercial Road.

ABOVE: Southampton West Station *c.,* 1908. This LSWR express may have carried White Star Line's London bound passengers just landed from the pride of their fleet, the 25,000 ton *Adriatic*. The latter was at the time, the largest vessel in the world.

ABOVE: This fine aerial view dates from 1904 and shows Southampton's western shoreline. In the foreground can be seen the municipal swimming pool and baths.

ABOVE: An imaginative card produced for the American Line in 1920 indicating how frail the *Mayflower* was when compared to the pride of their fleet *New York*. In a very few years the American Line ship would itself be dwarfed by the new super liners.

ABOVE: Stag Gates *c.,* 1907. This imposing entrance to Lodge Road was removed in 1919 to allow for double tram lines. Portions of the masonry ended up in East Park as pediments for flower stands and were used in the rockery near the *Titanic* memorial. The wrought iron gates were moved to the Old Cemetary.

ABOVE: The Arch, Weston *c.,* 1906. The Arch was built by Lord Radstock to connect one side of his estate with the other. It was demolished in the late 1930's. This view is looking towards Southampton Water along Weston Lane.

ABOVE: A fine, rural view of the Sun Hotel in Weston Lane around 1906. This spot is now the site of Squires Walk. Francis Godolphin Osborne Stuart was one of Southampton's finest photographers and postcard publishers. He operated from his Cromwell Road studio in Southampton for forty years.

ABOVE: Swaythling *c.,* 1905. This must have been a very quiet place to live in those days. Real development came with the formation of the Swaythling Housing Society in 1925. The purchase of eight acres of farmland near Wide Lane leading down to the Itchen River, started off the development.

TOP LEFT: Again from the 1950's, this is one of the shiny new vans of the South Hants Motor Company who were situated in St Mary's Street at the time. Ford had already gained a major foothold in the motor industry, and there were several Ford dealers dotted about the area offering spares and repair facilities, Hendy Lennox of course still proclaim themselves as Britain's 'first' Ford dealer.

ABOVE: This scene was taken at Eastleigh Airport, and shows Squire's, who were Southampton–based fruit brokers and importers, loading up their lorry direct from the plane's hold. Eastleigh Airport has recently been taken over by a private company who intend to make considerable improvements to both the services and the ageing fabric of many of the facilities.

BOTTOM LEFT: This van–driver surveys the damage after his van has taken a flying leap into a bomb site. Onlookers manage to keep straight faces, but do not seem too keen on assisting the unfortunate driver.

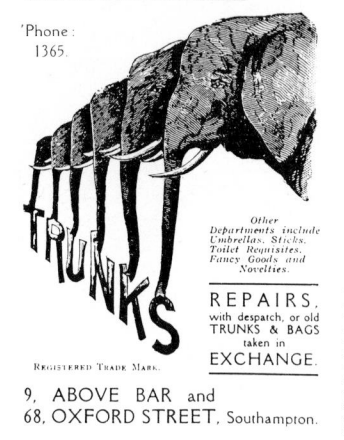

ABOVE: Co−author, Peter Boyd-Smith's grandfather standing beside the lorry that he drove for the Foundry Lane based Palmer's Steam Laundry, seen in Marsh Lane in the late 1920's.

TOP RIGHT: The Cunard *Queens* were always a big attraction when they were in port, and Star Boats were keen to exploit this with tours around the docks from the Royal Pier for 2/6d.

BOTTOM RIGHT: Throughout the 1950's, Southampton's position as the world's premier passenger port remained unchallenged. At the start of the decade a new 'Ocean Terminal' was built to provide modern and elegant passenger accommodation and to replace the original two storey sheds. The terminal, seen here under construction, could handle up to 2000 passengers on the upper floor. The ground floor was used for boat−trains, cargo, cars and office space. The passenger accommodation boasted a wooden panelled interior decorated in Art Deco style. The terminal was demolished in 1982, amid much local debate about other possible uses which could have been found for this large and historic building.

DESIGNED AND CONSTRUCTED BY
THE SUPERMARINE AVIATION WORKS LTD.
PROPRIETORS VICKERS (AVIATION) LIMITED.

SUPERMARINE ROLLS-ROYCE S.6. Winner of Schneider Trophy 1929. The Worlds speed record of 357.7 m.p.h. was accomplished with the same machine.

TOP LEFT: This photograph shows P & O's *Strathnaver* of 22,270 tons, together with a Short *Singapore* flying boat, in Southampton Water in the early 1930's. One wonders who had right of way?

ABOVE: The Supermarine factory was established on the banks of the River Itchen at Woolston in 1913. It gained a world–wide reputation in the 1930's with the advent of the famous Schneider Trophy races won by craft built at the factory. It was the engineering and design birthplace of the *Spitfire*, and consequently a prime target for Hitler's bombs in the blitz of the Second World War.

BOTTOM LEFT: The forerunner of the *Spitfire*, was the *Supermarine Rolls Royce S6* seaplane. Winner of the coveted Schneider Trophy in 1929, and holder of the world airspeed record of 357.7 mph. An *S6* plane can now be seen in the City's aviation museum opposite Ocean Village, along with a *Spitfire*.

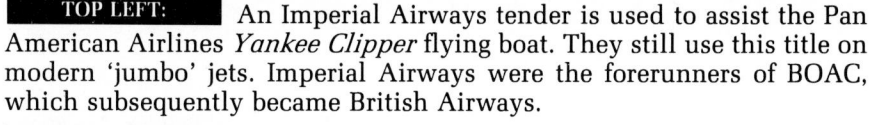

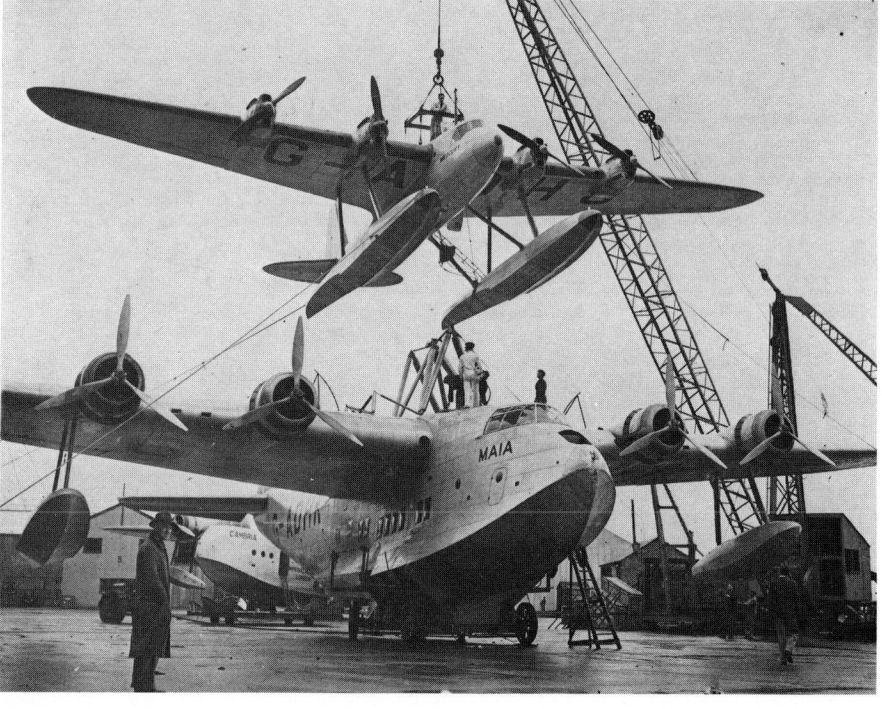

TOP LEFT: An Imperial Airways tender is used to assist the Pan American Airlines *Yankee Clipper* flying boat. They still use this title on modern 'jumbo' jets. Imperial Airways were the forerunners of BOAC, which subsequently became British Airways.

ABOVE: In 1938, the flying boat terminal was situated at the far end of the docks at berth 108. A two–storey wooden building was erected nearby and named rather grandly as Imperial House, after the airline that used it.

BOTTOM LEFT: Imperial Airway's technical adviser, R. H. Mayo, came up with a unique solution for flying mail across the Atlantic. He devised the Mayo composite aircraft, where a floatplane called *Mercury* was carried piggy–back on a larger plane. As the smaller plane did not use any fuel for take off, it could carry up to 1000 lb of mail. The first commercial usage of this service took place on 21st July 1938, when *Mercury* was launched over Dundee to fly non–stop to South Africa — a distance of 6,045 miles.

BRITISH OVERSEAS AIRWAYS CORPORATION

TELEPHONE : SOUTHAMPTON 3811

TELEGRAPHIC ADDRESS : SPEEDBIRD, SOUTHAMPTON

MARINE AIRPORT
BERTH 50
CANUTE ROAD
SOUTHAMPTON

29th April, 1948.

Captain H.W.C.Alger, Manager No.4 Line,
Hythe, and Mr.H.J.Bingham, Station
Superintendent, Southampton, request the
pleasure of the company of:

CAPTAIN A.E. BARTLETT

at a party at the Marine Airport, Berth 50,
Southampton Docks, on May 4th at 1130 LST
to inaugurate the "Solent" Flying-Boat
Service to South Africa (Departing 1145 LST)
and to a fork luncheon afterwards.

SOUTHAMPTON HARBOUR BOARD
★ 30 APR 1948 ★
HARBOUR MASTER'S OFFICE

R.S.V.P.   By telephone to:
                Miss Baker,
                Secretary to S/S.
                (Extension 2)

BOTTOM LEFT: Flying boat services returned to Southampton in March 1948. The Solent Class flying boat seen here was christened the *Southampton* by the Mayoress on 14th April, which also saw the formal opening of the new air terminal at berth 50 in the old docks.

ABOVE: A View of Southampton's air terminal. In his speech during the opening ceremony, the Minister of Aviation, Lord Nathan, outlined the fact that there could be problems ahead. He was right — only Britain continued to use the big flying boats. Others turned to the faster land planes. This meant that BOAC were forced to carry the entire running costs for their terminals, as no one else needed to use the facilities. Note the Royal Pier in the background.

CHAPTER TWO

Southampton, Ships and the Sea

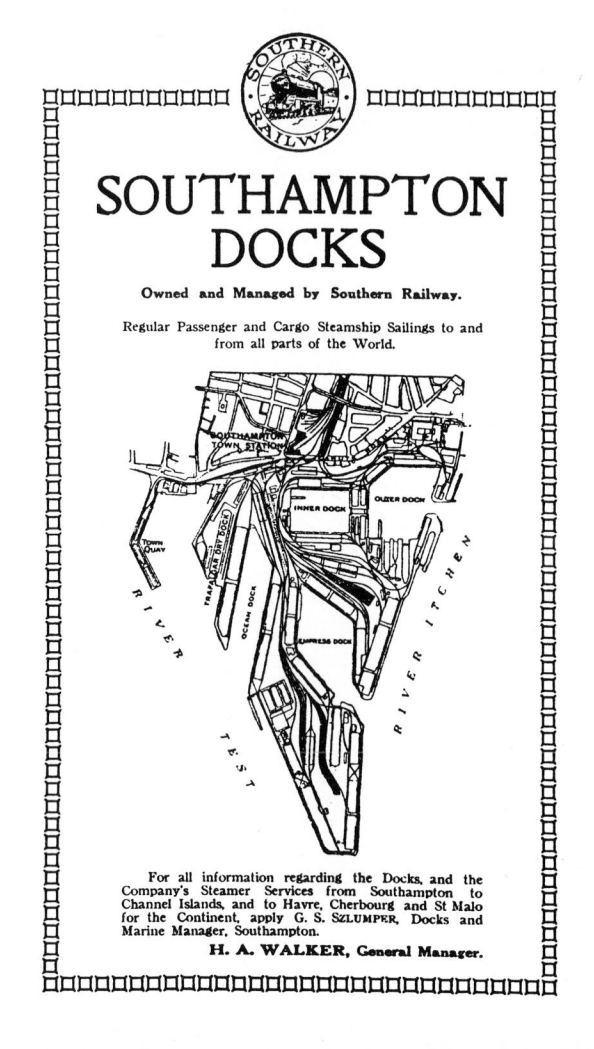

SOUTHAMPTON DOCKS

ROYAL PIER, SOUTHAMPTON.

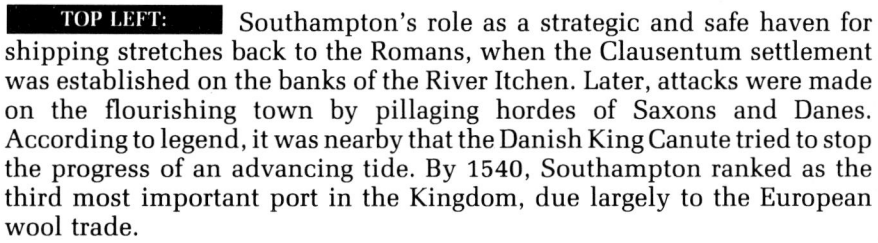

TOP LEFT: Southampton's role as a strategic and safe haven for shipping stretches back to the Romans, when the Clausentum settlement was established on the banks of the River Itchen. Later, attacks were made on the flourishing town by pillaging hordes of Saxons and Danes. According to legend, it was nearby that the Danish King Canute tried to stop the progress of an advancing tide. By 1540, Southampton ranked as the third most important port in the Kingdom, due largely to the European wool trade.

ABOVE: This photograph shows Woolston shipyard in the 1880's. A major boost to ship repairing and building took place a few years earlier in this area, when Thomas Ridley Oswald established a yard here. He had already been successful in his shipbuilding career up in Sunderland, where he had built 149 ships. He came to Southampton against the trend at the time, which was then centred on the Clyde. The first vessel he built at Woolston was an 853 ton, iron sailing ship called the *Aberfoyle*. He took on a partner called Henry Mordaunt, and the name of the company subsequently changed to Oswald Mordaunt. Between 1876, and 1889, the yard launched just over 100 vessels.

BOTTOM LEFT: In 1805, the Harbour Commission took over the running of the port, and one of their first major projects was the construction of the pier. It was built chiefly to accommodate steam packets which were operating to France, the Channel Islands and the Isle of Wight.

THE PIER

TOP LEFT: The newly formed Harbour Commissioners sought advice from the celebrated engineer, John Rennie, on ways of improving the quay. He attended a meeting on 5th June 1805, and it was decided that he should prepare a detailed report with the help of John Doswell, a Southampton surveyor, about constructing a new quay wall. It was Doswell who later undertook plans for the proposed new pier.

ABOVE: The contract for the construction of the wooden pier was given to a prominent local builder William Betts, who was also closely involved with the floating bridge scheme at Woolston. The pier took about six months to build, and was opened on 8th July 1833 by Princess Victoria, an event witnessed by over 2000 invited guests. The structure was originally called the Royal Victoria Pier. But there were problems — within five years, the timber piles had begun to rot (due to attack by a creature called a gribble) so badly that Doswell had to build an entirely new foundation to keep the pier safe. He covered the piles with thousands of large—headed iron nails, which were intended to rust and form a protective layer around the wood and hence keep the gribbles at bay. Both the pier itself, and the Harbour Board offices at nearby Town Quay, shown here, had distinctive domed roofs.

BOTTOM LEFT: Doswell put several alternative schemes for the pier before the Harbour Commissioners. One was for a stone structure at an estimated cost of some £14,000. Another was for a wooden one at almost half that figure. Consequently, the cheaper option was chosen, an Act enabling the construction was given Royal Assent on 30th July 1831.

THE ESPLANADE, SOUTHAMPTON.

S 2486 THE EMPRESS DOCK, SOUTHAMPTON.

AMERICAN LINE. SOUTHAMPTON—CHERBOURG—NEW YORK.

Twin Screw United States Mail Steamers
"NEW YORK"—"PHILADELPHIA"

TOP LEFT: This *c.*1927 photograph shows the Western Esplanade. The Cannons were brought back from the Crimean War, and several generations of children must have played on them before they were removed just before the Second World War. The sea used, of course to come right up to the walls at this point.

ABOVE: A. M. Rendell, the docks engineer, was commissioned to prepare a report on a proposed extension to the docks, to a length of 1,750 feet, providing berths for four large steamers. This was blocked when Alfred Giles, the Dock Company's engineer, put forward an alternative plan that comprised a new 16 acre dock site with 3,300 feet of quay. The corporation prepared a Bill to raise the money so that it could be lent to the Dock Company, their shareholders were less than sympathetic at seeing an already large burden of debt get any larger. The L&SWR came to the rescue with a loan which totalled £250,000, and meant construction of the new Empress Dock could be commenced. It was opened on 26th July 1890 by Queen Victoria.

BOTTOM LEFT: The steamship *City of Paris*, was originally launched on October 20th 1888, and sailed on her maiden voyage on April 3rd 1889, gaining the Blue Riband the next month. She was constructed for the Inman Line, but subsequently purchased by the American Line in 1893 and renamed *Paris*, providing accommodation for 290 first cass passengers, 250 second class and 725 steerage, with the ship weighing in at 10,508 tons. In 1898, she served briefly as a cruiser in the Spanish American war under the name of *Yale*. The following year she ran aground off Cornwall, causing damage that took five months to repair. When she re−entered service on August 31st, it was as *Philadelphia*, but there was to be another name change when, in 1917, she served the U.S. Navy for two years as an armed transport known as *Harrisburg*. Her life came to an end when, in 1923, she was finally broken up in Genoa.

ABOVE: *Philadephia* had a sister ship, built originally for the Inman Line, and christened *City of New York*. There was accommodation on board for 540 first class passengers, 200 second class, and 1000 steerage. She was launched on March 15th 1888, and sailed on her maiden voyage on August 1st. In 1893, she was taken over by the American Line and her name shortened simply to *New York*. Her first voyage in her new guise was from Southampton to New York on March 11th 1893. Five years later, she served as an auxiliary cruiser for the U.S. Navy in the Spanish American war under the name *Harvard*, before being refitted in 1901, emerging with two instead of the original three funnels. With the outbreak of war, she entered service on the New York to Liverpool route, and also served the navy once more, this time as an armed cruiser, under the name *Plattsburg*. It was 1919 before she once again became the *New York* of the American Line, operating for just over a year before being sold to the Polish Navigation Company and working the New York — Mediterranean route, before being broken up, like her sister ship, in Genoa in 1923.

BOTTOM LEFT: The White Star liner *Titanic*. This photograph shows her leaving Southampton docks, proudly embarking on her maiden voyage as the largest vessel in the world. A few days later the name *Titanic* would be synonymous with death, disaster and doom. The ship collided with an iceberg and the tragedy claimed 1,523 lives. The disaster did, however, force through new safety rules and navigation principles which all ships have benefited from since. But what a terrible price to pay for such change. Over 600 Southampton families were affected by the loss of the *Titanic* on 10th April 1912.

UNION CASTLE LINER LEAVING SOUTHAMPTON. 137.

1970. F. G. O. Stuart.   THE WHITE STAR DOCK. SOUTHAMPTON.

7104. The Empress of Australia & Empress of Britain berthed at New Docks, Southampton.

TOP LEFT: An enthusiastic farewell for a Union Castle Liner, leaving Southampton during the First World War. *c.,*1916.

ABOVE: The *Empress of Australia* (right), and *Empress of Britain* berthed at Southampton's New Western Docks. The *Empress of Australia* was originally laid down as the German liner, *Tirpitz*. Work on her was halted during the First World War, and she was handed over to Britain following the conflict in 1920, before being sold the following year to Canadian Pacific, and re–named the *Empress of China*. Then, in 1922, another name change, this time to *Empress of Australia*. On September 1st 1923, she was almost destroyed during the great Tokyo earthquake. The first tremor smashed the Yokohama pier from which the ship was just putting out, and she swirled through the harbour completely out of control and collided with a Japanese cargo vessel before drifting helplessly towards a blazing oilfield. Luckily, she was towed clear by a Dutch tanker. Throughout the years between the wars, she operated between Southampton and Quebec, before finally becoming a troop transport, as she remained after the war until she was broken up in 1952.

ABOVE: In 1907, the White Star Line's service was transferred from Liverpool to Southampton. In honour of this, a new 15½ acre deep water dock was opened in 1911, and named after the company. Following the attraction to Southampton of other line's ships, the name of this was changed, in 1922, to the Ocean Dock. To deal with the cargoes of these massive ships, 16 electric cranes were installed.

THE LARGEST FLOATING DOCK IN THE WORLD, SOUTHAMPTON

2143. F. G. O. Stuart.   THE FLOATING DRY-DOCK, SOUTHAMPTON.
THE LARGEST FLOATING DRY-DOCK IN THE WORLD.

TOP LEFT: This floating dock was designed by Clark & Standfield and constructed by Armstrong Whitworth Ltd at Newcastle, before being opened by HRH the Prince of Wales on 27th June 1924. At this time, it was the largest of its kind in the world. It was 960 feet long, with a 134 feet wide entrance, with a draft of water over the keel blocks of 38 feet. It would hold vessels up to 60,000 tons. At that time, the *Majestic*, which was the largest liner afloat, weighed in at just over 52,000 tons. The floating system was much cheaper than a conventional dry dock, but with the launching of Cunard's *Queen Mary* of over 80,000 tons, it became of limited use.

ABOVE: The floating dock covered an area of some 3½ acres, and had 16,000 tons of steel in its hull, put together with four million rivets. The height of the dock from the bottom of the pontoon, to the top deck was over 70 feet. It was made of seven separate sections which could be dismantled and docked separately for repair. The pumps had to deliver ten 18 inch diameter streams of water, and four 15 inch diameter streams at a velocity of 10 feet per second constantly for four hours, to drain the dock.

BOTTOM LEFT: A well−loved liner often seen dominating the Southampton docks skyline was the four−funnelled *Mauretania* of the Cunard Line. She was built by Swan Hunter & Wigham Richardson and measured some 790 × 88 feet. There was accommodation for 560 first class passengers, 475 second class and 1,300 third, together with 812 crew members. Launching took place on September 20th 1906, and her maiden voyage was from Liverpool to New York on November 16th 1907. Until 1911, she was the biggest ship in the world.

THE OCEAN DOCK, SOUTHAMPTON.

2158. F. G. O. Stuart.

1203 C. R. Hoffmann AERIAL VIEW OF SOUTHAMPTON DOCKS, SHOWING NINE OF THE WORLD'S LARGEST LINERS. Southampton. GROSS TONNAGE 316,000 TONS.

ABOVE: This remarkable aerial view of Southampton Docks shows nine of the world's largest liners, and emphasises the City's lead in maritime handling. This photograph dates from the early 1930's and shows a total gross tonnage of 316,000 tons of passenger shipping. By comparison the *QE2* of today has a gross tonnage of 65,000 tons.

BOTTOM LEFT: The beautiful French liner, *Normandie* was 1030 × 117.8 feet, and had accommodation for 848 first class passengers, 670 tourist class, and 454 third class, together with 1,345 crew. She was launched on October 29th 1932, and was the biggest ship in the world until 1940, when the *Queen Elizabeth* entered service. Her maiden voyage was on 29th May 1935 from Le Havre to New York, during which she won the Blue Riband with an average speed of 29.98 knots, then broke the record again on the return journey with an average of 30.31 knots. In 1939, she was laid up because of the threat of war, and siezed by the US Maritime Commission on December 12th, 1941, and renamed *Lafayette*. During conversion work in February 1942, a fire started on the promenade deck and spread quickly across the upper decks. Water was pumped relentlessly on board, but this only succeeded in making the ship top heavy, and she eventually keeled over. She was righted on August 7th 1943, and plans were drawn up for her conversion to an aircraft carrier, but this was not to be, and after the war, the wreck was sold by the US Maritime Commission as scrap.

S.S. Normandie.

TOP LEFT: A pre–war view of the Ocean Dock, from ground level. Nowadays, the three and four funnelled mammoths have all gone, and the tradition is maintained by just two superliners — the *QE2*, and P & O's *Canberra*.

The Canadian Pacific Super-Liner "EMPRESS OF BRITAIN."

Launched by H.R.H. The Prince of Wales, June 11th, 1930, at Clydebank Shipyard, Glasgow, the Canadian Pacific "EMPRESS OF BRITAIN" is the largest vessel of the Canadian Pacific Fleet of seventy-eight splendid ships. In service summer of 1931, between Southampton and Quebec, the "EMPRESS OF BRITAIN" will be the biggest ship to ply between any two ports of the British Empire—42,500 tons.

The vessel is to maintain an average sea speed of 24 knots. She has a straight stem raking well forward, and a cruiser stern, and has three funnels and two pole masts. The funnels are of the pear-shaped section, and measure about 27 feet across the widest part and 35 feet fore and aft. They are about 68 feet high above the Sun Deck. The masts measure about 208 feet above the Load Water Line, and are the longest masts yet constructed at the Clydebank Yard.

The ship has a continuous Shelter Deck over the Upper Deck, a Bridge Deck over Shelter Deck, extending the full length of the vessel, a Promenade Deck over the Shelter Deck for more than three-fourths the length of the vessel, a Boat Deck over the Promenade Deck, for over half the length of the ship, and a Sun Deck over this Boat Deck.

She will be built to the requirements of the highest class of Lloyd's Registry under special survey, 100 A1, subdivided by water-tight bulkheads and fully equipped with all life-saving appliances to comply with latest requirements of the International Convention for the Safety of Life at Sea. In every respect, this vessel will be finished in the best style as a First-Class Atlantic Passenger steamer of the highest type.

The "Empress of Britain" will have quadruple screws, single reduction turbines and high pressure watertube boilers, and will be the largest and most important installation yet constructed with high pressure steam machinery as the motive power.

Beautifully decorated by famous artists, the public rooms of the "Empress of Britain" will include :—

Dining-room ; Private Dining-rooms ; Lounge ; Ballroom ; Smoking-room ; Writing-room ; Card-room ; Long Gallery ; American Bar ; Swimming-bath and Cafe ; Turkish Bath ; Gymnasium ; Squash Racquet Court ; Tennis Court and Cafe ; Children's Room ; Children's Gymnasium ; Hairdressers' Shops ; Beauty Parlours ; Shop ; Flower Stall, etc.

The passenger accommodation has been planned on the most modern and up-to-date lines, a particular feature of the First-Class Staterooms being that all these are outside rooms, having direct light through the ship's side. The Tourist Third Cabin Staterooms are based on the Cabin Staterooms of the "Duchess" class of steamers, and the Third Class are superior to anything yet fitted for that type of passenger.

All the First-Class Staterooms will be fitted with bedsteads of large size, large dressing-tables having cabinet on top with triple folding mirrors, a fitted wardrobe for each passenger, a large settee, a dressing-table stool, an arm-chair and an easy chair and bedside tables, also a full-length wall mirror, cabinet for toilet requisites, means for securing wardrobe trunks, etc.

In addition to the amenities already cited, there are a thousand worth indicating, of which only a few can be mentioned here. There are exquisite beauty parlours for the ladies, and a barber's shop for men ; an up-to-date novelty shop and flower-stall ; and telephone rooms communicating with the shore during the entire voyage.

On board the "Empress of Britain" no lover of sport need lapse in his form. Covered with wire-netting, the open-air tennis court on the boat-deck aft is of full size for doubles, with plenty of over-run space. The squash racquet court is suited for championship matches. Both courts have galleries for spectators. There is a fully equipped gymnasium which leads to the swimming-bath. This is framed on a scale surpassing all Atlantic records. The surroundings include glass mosaic columns under a glass roof, woodwork of carven teak, and a spectators' gallery, the bath being served by lifts. Water comes continuously from a monster turtle fashioned of terrazzo glass, and perpetual daylight is afforded by hidden lights, with brilliant floodlights under the water.

There is a spacious sports deck on the top of the vessel amidships, and exclusive of the tennis court and sports deck, the area of promenade deck for first class alone measures 26,000 ft., or the extent of a moderate fairway on an average golf course.

The vessel will be equipped with wireless telegraphy and direction-finding apparatus, wireless telephony, submarine signalling apparatus, gyro compass equipment, electric submerged log, echo-sounding machine, electric orchestra and gramophone repeater installation, talkie cinema apparatus, electric vacuum cleaning plant, electric clocks, burglar alarms, electric loudspeaking telephones, inter-communicating telephones, electric bells, alarm booters, fire alarms, semaphores and morse lamps, clear-view screens, and many other electric appliances.

Searchlights, range-finders, and other up-to-date appliances are installed on the captain's bridge, and in this atmosphere of Safety First and Last the skipper and his officers command every department of a vessel unsurpassed by anything building or built.

The "EMPRESS OF BRITAIN" will provide a new and shorter route to New York and other points in the United States. The time from Southampton to New York will be only 5 days

"EMPRESS OF BRITAIN."

BRITAIN'S Latest Shipbuilding Achievement, the CANADIAN PACIFIC Super-liner "EMPRESS OF BRITAIN," as she will appear when in service on June 17, 1931, from Southampton to Quebec, the largest and fastest ship between any two ports of the British Empire. The "EMPRESS OF BRITAIN" was launched by H.R.H. The Prince of Wales, at Clydebank, Glasgow, on June 11, 1930, to be the Flagship of the Canadian Pacific Fleet of 78 steamships. Her length is 758 ft., breadth 97 ft. 6 in., depth 60 ft. 9 in., tonnage 42,500 and speed 24 knots.

She will sail on an Enchanting World Cruise in Nov. 1931

ASK THE CANADIAN PACIFIC—62-65 Charing Cross LONDON S.W.1

TOP LEFT: The *Empress of Britain*, seen here at Southampton Docks, was Canadian Pacific's largest passenger ship. She was built on the Clyde, and had accommodation for 465 first class passengers, 260 tourist class, and 470 third class. She carried 740 crew and was launched on June 11th 1930, sailing on her maiden voyage from Southampton to Quebec on May 27th. In the war, she was converted to a troop transport, and on October 26th 1940, bound from Canada to England, she was attacked by a German long—range bomber 70 miles off Ireland and set on fire. Passengers and crew luckily had time to take to boats, and were picked up by naval vessels. Although the liner was burning, she was still afloat, and was taken in tow by a Polish destroyer, but then a German submarine finished her off with two torpedoes on October 28th.

ABOVE: A Canadian Pacific advertising poster from 1931, when the *Empress of Britain* was the pride of the line.

ABOVE: "The world's largest liner enters the world's largest graving dock", or so they said on 19th January 1934 when this photograph was taken. The White Star Liner, *Majestic*, has successfully entered the King George V Graving Dock, which was built to accommodate vessels up to 100,000 tons.

TOP LEFT: The *Queen Mary* and her sister ship *Queen Elizabeth* are by far the most popular of Southampton's ships. *Queen Mary* was built for Cunard by Browns on the Clyde. On May 27th 1936, she sailed from Southampton to New York on her maiden voyage, winning the Blue Riband back from *Normandie* with an average speed of 30.14 knots. She measured 1,019 × 118 feet and had accommodation for 776 cabin class passengers, 784 tourist class and 579 third class, together with 1,101 crew members. In 1939, she was laid up at New York because of war, and subsequently converted into a troop transport, being fitted out in Sydney, Australia. On October 2nd 1942 on a voyage from America to the Clyde, the ship was being escorted by the British cruiser *Curacoa*, which came under the bows of the *Mary* as she sailed a zig–zag course at full speed. The small cruiser was sliced in half, resulting in the deaths of 338 of the 439 crew members. Her first post–war voyage took place on July 31st 1947, and she remained in service until 1967 when, on August 18th, she was sold to the City of Long Beach, California. On May 10th 1971, after a massive conversion programme, she was opened to the public.

ABOVE: This photograph was taken on 27th July 1938, and shows the *Queen Mary* in the King George V dry dock in the new docks. Land reclamation is complete and the in–fill is gradually being covered by buildings. The dock had been opened by King George V, the day before this shot was taken, and was the largest dry dock in the world. It could accommodate vessels up to 100,000 tons. Its construction involved the excavation of 750,000 tons of earth. Following which, some three quarters of a million tons of concrete were used for the walls and floor.

34

ABOVE: A general view of the docks on the 14th June 1949, showing *Queen Mary*, in her nice bright house colours after being a drab, camouflage grey throughout the war years. The building undergoing construction is the Ocean Terminal which was sadly demolished in the early 1980's.

TOP RIGHT: The Ocean terminal was opened in 1951 to provide a modern style of passenger accommodation in place of the original single storey sheds, and could handle 2000 passengers. As can be seen from this photograph, the passenger area was wood panelled in an art deco style, in keeping with the *Queen Mary* and *Queen Elizabeth* interiors. It represented a fitting welcome for film stars and heads of state in the heady years of post— war optimism.

BOTTOM RIGHT: The *United States* in Southampton. This liner measured 990 × 101.7 feet, and had accommodation for 871 first class passengers, 508 cabin class, and 549 tourist class, together with 1,093 crew. She was delivered on June 21st 1952 to United States Line, and embarked upon her maiden voyage from New York to Southampton on July 3rd. She broke all Atlantic speed records, with an average speed on her homeward voyage of 34.51 knots — a record yet to be broken by a cruise liner, making her the fastest commercial ship ever built. She continued in service, struggling with the commercial threat of the jet airliner, until November 8th 1969, when she was laid up. She was subsequently bought by the US Maritime Administration.

ABOVE: Gater's Hill, West End *c.,* 1905. This scene has changed little since this photograph was taken, although the White Swan pub has recently had a facelift.

ABOVE: Tanner's Brook, Millbrook *c.,* 1920. A tanyard or leatherworks, operated here for well over 100 years. Higher density housing now occupies the whole of this area which is bounded by Tebourba Way and King George's Avenue.

ABOVE: The Cowherds, Southampton Common *c.,* 1905. A popular traveller's rest on the way into Southampton from Winchester. It was originally the home of the Cowherd who looked after the Common on behalf of the town. It was first used as an inn early in the 19th Century, the rent going to the Corporation. Coronation Avenue begins here on its path across the Common.

ABOVE: Shirley Warren *c.,* 1906. The Southampton Incorporation Infirmary in what was originally known as Chilworth Road, now Tremona Road.

ABOVE: Bitterne *c.,* 1904. This is a view of Pound Street, in the foreground the actual pound itself where lost cattle and the like were held pending return to their owners or possibly a drover would collect 'beasts' from here for the journey into Southampton. Bursledon Road heads away to the right from the centre of the picture, to the left the Red Lion pub.

ABOVE: Woolston from the Floating Bridge *c.,* 1907. A seemingly informal view of Portsmouth Road showing the original toll house on the right. The waiting room and small 'Coffee Tavern' plus the toll house are now sadly no more but modern Woolston can be easily discerned from this photograph.

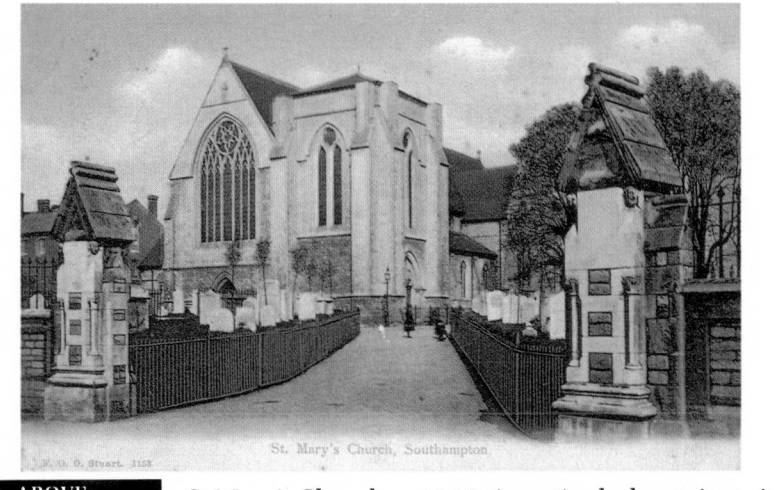

ABOVE: St Mary's Church *c.,* 1906. A particularly ancient site of worship, this building was completed in 1884 and stands as a memorial to one of Southampton's most notable churchmen Canon Wilberforce, grandson of the anti-slavery campaigner. It was designed by Mr G. E. Street and opened by Edward Prince of Wales.

ABOVE: Southampton West Station *c.,* 1907. This was the approximate site of Blechynden Station (now Southampton Central), it was connected with the London line in 1847. The Corporation saved the town centre parks by insisting on a much longer tunnel than originally planned, the deepest parts dug by Cornish tin miners, but mostly constructed by the 'cut and cover' method.

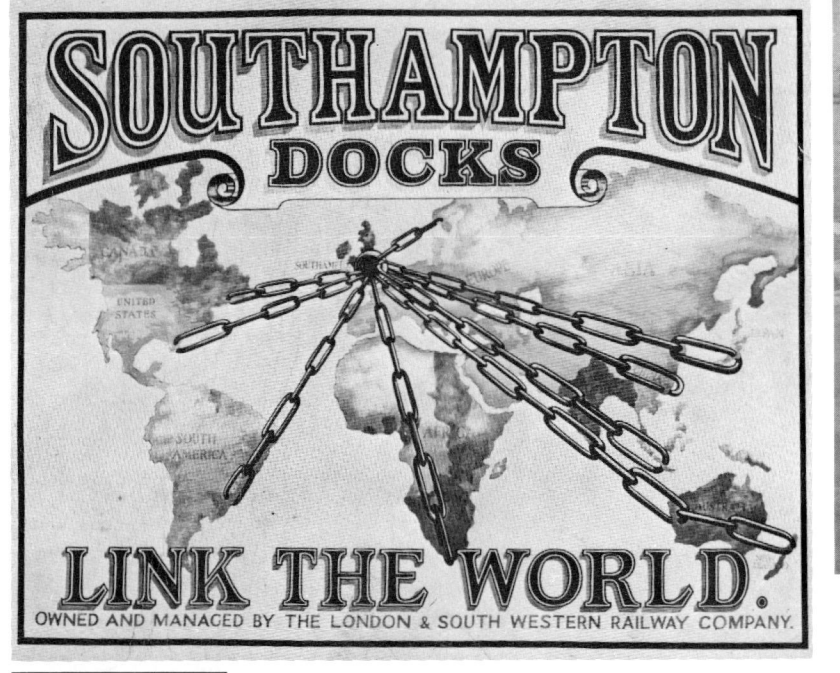

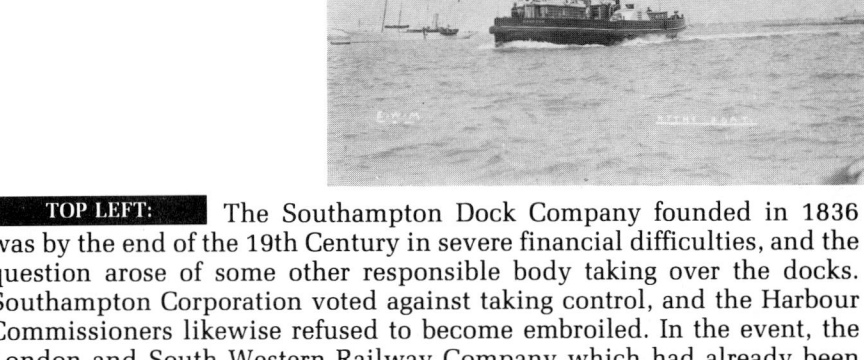

TOP RIGHT: The *Queen Elizabeth*, seen here alongside Southampton's Ocean Terminal in 1965, was the largest passenger ship ever built. She was constructed by Browns on the Clyde and measured 1,029 × 118.4 feet, and had accommodation for 823 first class passengers, 662 cabin class, and 798 tourist class, together with 1,296 crew members. She was launched on September 27th 1938, and, almost complete, on February 28th 1940, she dashed across the Atlantic to be safe from the threat of attack from the Luftwaffe — a story was circulated at the time to confuse the enemy that she was heading for Southampton. Once safely at New York, she was laid up, before being converted to a troop transport in November in Sydney. She was released from her war service and sailed on her first real maiden voyage on October 16th 1946, on the Southampton to New York route. She was overhauled in late 1965, but rather suddenly Cunard decided that she was to be withdrawn from service. She sailed from Southampton for the last time on December 8th 1968 bound for Port Everglades. The ship was eventually bought by a Japanese businessman, C. Y. Tung, who registered her in Hong Kong as the *Seawise University*. The ship sailed from Port Everglades to Hong Kong on July 16th 1971, being held up several times with boiler trouble. Just as the old Queen's future looked assured, a fire broke out during the last part of her refit and the next day, she ship heeled over in the harbour, a total wreck.

TOP LEFT: The Southampton Dock Company founded in 1836 was by the end of the 19th Century in severe financial difficulties, and the question arose of some other responsible body taking over the docks. Southampton Corporation voted against taking control, and the Harbour Commissioners likewise refused to become embroiled. In the event, the London and South Western Railway Company which had already been loaning large sums of money to the Dock Company anyway, purchased the site in 1892. It proved an excellent investment there was considerable prosperity just around the corner — by 1927 Southampton claimed to be the country's premier passenger port.

ABOVE: It wasn't only superliners that populated Southampton docks during its heyday — there were some smaller craft that were just as important! This photograph shows a police launch from about 1954. It could often be seen patrolling the waters of the Itchen and the Test.

BOTTOM RIGHT: The Hythe–Southampton paddle steamer *Hampton*, owned and operated by the Percy family crossing the mouth of the River Test in about 1910, this is a card from the Ashlett Studio of Edward Mudge.

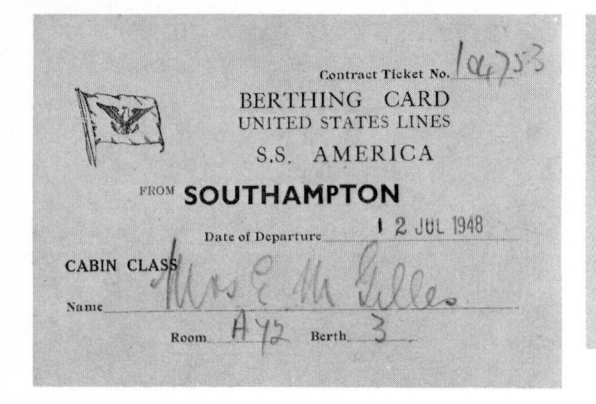

Contract Ticket No. 104753

BERTHING CARD
UNITED STATES LINES
S.S. AMERICA

FROM **SOUTHAMPTON**

Date of Departure 1 2 JUL 1948

CABIN CLASS Mrs E M Gilles

Name

Room A72 Berth 3

SOUTHAMPTON TOWN QUAY CRUISES
around the Port give you
the BEST VIEW of the Docks and

"Wonder Ships" "of the World"

BOATS FOR HIRE,
COACH PARTIES,
SCHOOLS,
FISHING, ETC.

PRIVATE PARTIES,
WORKS
OUTINGS,
ETC.

"SOUTHAMPTON TOWN QUAY CRUISES"
Continuous Docks Cruising Service from the Town Quay
TELEPHONE 74465 — 24145 SOUTHAMPTON

The Directors of
John I. Thornycroft & Co Limited
request the pleasure of the company of

Captain & Mrs. A.E. Bartlett.

at the launch of
"Commandant Queré"
by
Madame Albert Lellouche
at Woolston Works, Southampton,
on Saturday, 29th November, 1947, at 11a.m.
Owing to catering restrictions a buffet luncheon will
be served in the Woolston Works after the ceremony.

R.S.V.P. to
Woolston Works.
Southampton.

(For travelling
arrangements please
see over)

Visit of
H.M.S. "ARK ROYAL"
and
U.S.S. "FORRESTAL"
TO
SOUTHAMPTON NEW DOCKS

September 30th to October 11th

Cheap tickets available from this station to Southampton Central daily

For further particulars see handbills

On the dates the ships are open to visitors admission will be at No. 10 Gate, Southampton Docks — approximately 400 yards from Southampton Central Station

BRITISH RAILWAYS

ABOVE: Advert card for Dock cruises.

TOP LEFT: Embarkation card stamped on the reverse by an immigration officer in Southampton.

TOP RIGHT: Poster issued by Southern Region for display at Waterloo in 1957.

CHAPTER THREE

The Villages Of Southampton

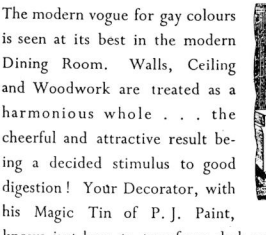

ROYAL VICTORIA HOSPITAL. NETLEY. S.C. 90.

Shirley High Street, Southampton. 4378.

TOP LEFT: Southampton became a centre for the embarkation and disembarkation of troops during the Crimean war. In fact, during the two years of conflict P & O alone transported over 100,000 men to the Crimea. Many came back wounded, and a new military hospital at Netley was planned. The new building was named in honour of Queen Victoria who laid the foundation stone on 19th May 1856. The design attracted criticism from Florence Nightingale who felt that medical principles had been sacrificed to the vanity of the architect. The area is now a country park, and little of the grandeur of the original site remains, the only surviving relic of this fine tribute to Victorian values is the central tower with its beautiful domed cupola.

ABOVE: Originally a common existed in Shirley, which lay between Hill Lane, Shirley Road, and the High Street. It was partly on this, and partly on the adjoining Millbrook Common, to the east of Shirley Road, that the suburb grew up. The first Lord of Shirley made an agreement with the people of Southampton in the reign of Henry III, which gave Southampton its common. The horse trough seen in this card has been moved several times, it now resides in the modern precinct on the corner of Anglesea Road and Shirley High Street.

BOTTOM LEFT: Shirley's original church is thought to have been destroyed in the middle of the fifteenth century, and until this new one was built, inhabitants were forced to make a journey by coach, horseback or on foot, to neighbouring Millbrook, for worship. This card dates from around 1905.

TOP LEFT: Portswood 1937. Always an important link in Southampton's transport system from the time that horse drawn trams were introduced in 1839 — the main depot was in the village, where the majority of space was taken up with stabling for over 100 horses. Today close to this site the modern Bus Garage and depot for City Bus is located, the tradition of public service to the people of Southampton continues. The street decorations seen here were for the Coronation celebrations for George VI.

ABOVE: A class gathering of group 4 of St Deny's Infants school in 1905. The village was once famous as being the site of one of the most noted of Southampton's ecclesiastical establishments — St Deny's Priory. There are those who say they have seen ghostly figures of the monks on dark, winter evenings haunting the environs of their former home.

BOTTOM LEFT: A class from St Patrick's Roman Catholic School in Woolston. The opening ceremony in 1884 was conducted by the Bishop of Portsmouth, the aptly named Reverend Monsignore Virtue, in the presence of a large congregation.

Woolston.

Portsmouth Arch.

The Wrench Series, No. 5380.

TOP LEFT: Woolston grew into a thriving community, aided by the shipbuilding that developed on the River Itchen, culminating in the opening of Thornycrofts yard. This is an early 1950's view of Portsmouth Road, the impact of billboard advertising is very evident.

ABOVE: Boots the chemists; Lankester & Crooks; Whitbreads ales — there are many famous names advertised down Victoria Road in Woolston in this photograph. The date, around 1938.

BOTTOM LEFT: The River Itchen in the background of this photograph was traversed by the floating bridge. Whilst the scene remains largely unchanged today, the river here is now dominated by the huge concrete road bridge, the date of this photograph is around 1905.

TOP LEFT: Housing development inevitably made calls on other areas of the City's resources and one of the results was Itchen Secondary School. This is an interior view of the English room and hard at work are Form VA in the Autumn of 1924.

ABOVE: An everyday occurrence at Itchen Secondary School in Merry Oak, and one no doubt looked forward to by the pupils — dinner hour. The hut was burnt down in December 1930. The school has now graduated to being a sixth form college.

BOTTOM LEFT: The East bank of the Itchen River became particularly desirable after Northam Bridge had been built in the 1790's. A number of rather grand properties were built here for the rich and famous, including this one, Peartree House, this photograph dates from 1905.

VIEW ON PEAR TREE GREEN

Weston, N. Southampton. 1029.

High St. Bitterne.

TOP LEFT: Peartree Green was the scene of a mock battle in 1804, when in preparation for the very real threat of a French invasion, local militia volunteers staged a seaborne attack on the Green from the nearby River Itchen.

ABOVE: The sleepy hamlet of Weston has changed beyond all recognition. The area was the first to be earmarked for overspill housing following the Second World War — 100 brick built houses were constructed and handed over to their proud new tenants in 1946.

BOTTOM LEFT: This view is of the High Street in Bitterne, at the turn of the century, and we are looking West. The iron hoop held by the smaller of the two girls in the centre of the picture would be bowled along with a short stick, a popular street game for young people of this time.

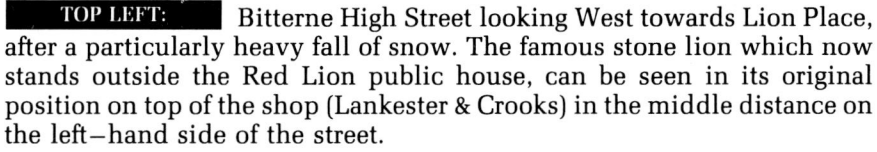

TOP LEFT: Bitterne High Street looking West towards Lion Place, after a particularly heavy fall of snow. The famous stone lion which now stands outside the Red Lion public house, can be seen in its original position on top of the shop (Lankester & Crooks) in the middle distance on the left—hand side of the street.

ABOVE: Highfield Lane in 1904. Ten years later, the buildings that had been constructed nearby as the University College, were taken over by the War Department as a military hospital to cope with injuries sustained in the Great War.

BOTTOM LEFT: Church Lane in Highfield. From the village's modest beginnings sprang a development based around the neighbouring Uplands Estate, which, by the 1930's, had resulted in the construction of some 200 houses and flats, built in picturesque settings, making the area highly desirable, as it remains to this day.

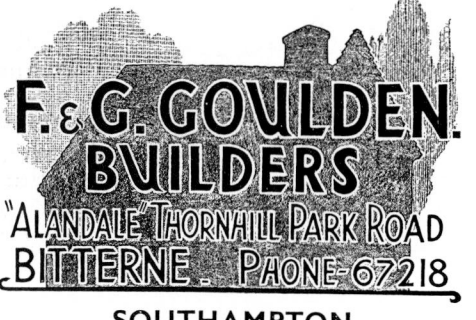
TOP LEFT: Woodmill in 1906. These days cars queue up along the same road to negotiate the narrow river bridge in single file. In the mid–18th century there was a block making works here, the proprietor, Walter Taylor, enjoyed a virtual monopoly for the supply of rigging blocks to the Navy.

ABOVE: Chafen Road in Bitterne Manor. This part of the City has grown up on land that once formed the Roman Clausentum settlement. There is archaeological evidence to suggest that the earliest extensive occupation took place as far back as the Flavian period around AD79. The Coachman's Lodge for Bitterne Manor can be seen in the left background, it was built for the MacNaghten family as part of their estate in the early 1800's.

Tanners Brook, Millbrook Road

Lodge Road, North, Southampton.   4294.

TOP LEFT: Millbrook Village. This scene was to change with post–war development, when the Corporation designed a "garden city" style housing estate that extended to the erection of 3,217 dwellings. In 1954, the Borough boundaries were moved to include parts of Millbrook for the first time. This photograph was taken in the mid–1930's.

ABOVE: This is believed to be the Four Posts mission at number 17 Millbrook Road, Millbrook. The photograph dates from around 1911.

BOTTOM LEFT: This view shows Lodge Road North, looking towards the rear of Stag Gates. The gates were originally built for William Betts, one of the last owners of the large estate, in about 1845. Shortly after this date, it was sold to Sampson Payne, an enterprising property speculator; the estate was then broken up for building by the Conservative Land Society.

The Clock Tower, Southampton

THE TRIANGLE
BITTERNE PARK, SOUTHAMPTON.

ABOVE: This clock tower, which included a drinking fountain, stood in a prominent position in Above Bar. It was bequeathed to the town by a Mrs Henrietta Bellenden Sayers in 1889. Almost directly opposite stood the London and South Western Railway Office.

TOP RIGHT: Same clock tower — different location! It was removed from Above Bar, and re−erected at Bitterne Triangle in March 1934 where it stands today. This photograph also features Elliots cycle shop which still trades on the same spot.

BOTTOM RIGHT: St Mary's College in Bitterne Park. The actual building remains but long gone are these traditional benches and desks. Note the window through to the adjoining classroom, a feature of many educational establishments of bygone ages, no doubt the map of Africa on the wall had a good deal of Empire 'red' on it at this time.

CHAPTER FOUR

The War Years

The Mayor's Parlour,
Civic Centre,
Southampton.
21st August, 1945.

Dear Captain Bartlett,

<u>Third Day's Holiday in connection with V.E. Day</u>
<u>10th September, 1945</u>

I am anxious to arrange a Regatta on the Weston Foreshore on the above date and I would be glad of your co-operation in this connection.

I have called an informal meeting for Thursday, 24th inst. at 6.30 p.m. in my Parlour and although I know this is rather short notice, I would be very glad indeed to see you then if you can possibly make it convenient to come along.

Yours sincerely,

J. C. Dyas

Capt. G. E. Bartlett,
63, Northam Avenue,
Southampton.

(J. C. Dyas)
Mayor.

VE + 2 DAY
Monday, 10th Sept., 1945

Sailing Events commencing at 12 noon
Rowing   „   „   „ 2.15 p.m.

OFF THE
WESTON FORESHORE
WOOLSTON

SUMMER ENTERTAINMENTS

REGATTA

President and Commodore—
The Worshipful the Mayor of Southampton (Councillor J. C. DYAS)
Vice Commodore—Mr. A. W. Axton
Rear-Commodore—Captain A. E. Bartlett

Southampton Sailing Committee—
Chairman—Lieut. B. J. Shelly Barter, R.N. (rtd.)
Hon. Secretary—Mr. A. C. Sanderson

Rowing Committee—
Chairman—Mr. B. Mortimer
Hon. Secretary—Mr. A. Chatfield

Swimming Committee—
Hon. Secretary—Mr. C. Bartlett

Rowing Officials—
Judges—Messrs. Ernest Lepard, A. Fraser, Capt. Bartlett
Starter—Mr. Bernard Mortimer
Competitors' Stewards and Recorders—Messrs. R. W. Gray, A. Chatfield
Stewards of Course—Messrs. Ernest Lepard, Councillor Lambeth

OFFICIAL PROGRAMME   **2D.**

ABOVE: An early card dated 1911 showing Southampton's very own 5th Battalion of The Hampshire Regiment (Territorial Force) on their annual Summer manoeuvres in deepest, darkest Dorset. These men are being allocated their 'outposts'. The regiment did not become 'Royal' until 1946. The original purchaser of this card posted it in Wareham to his sweetheart at home in Freemantle. Many of these men would have gone to France in 1914, perhaps even marching through the Bar Gate as generations of Britain's fighting men had done before.

RIGHT: A photograph dating from 1917, of Edwin and Annie Holley, with baby Iris. This was taken during Edwin's leave from the Western Front.

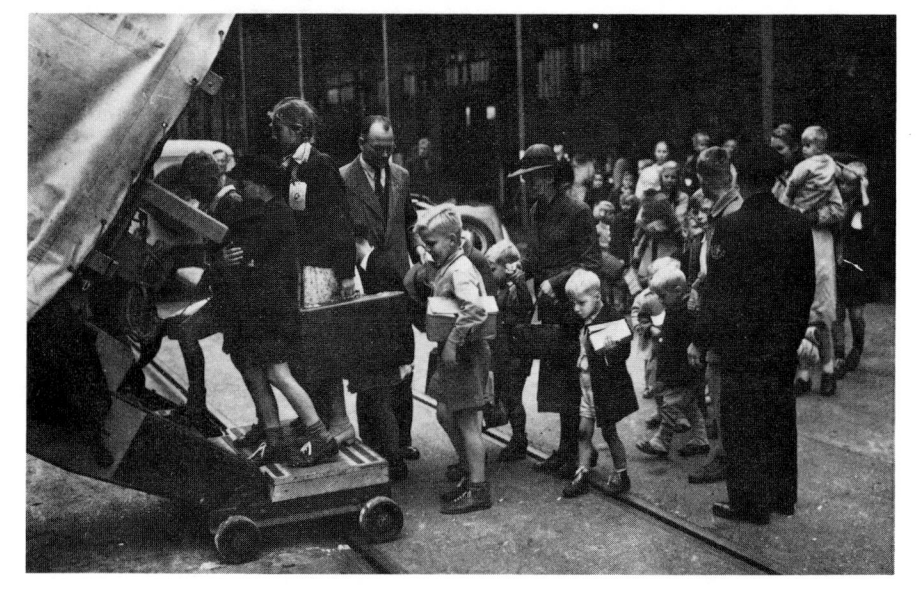

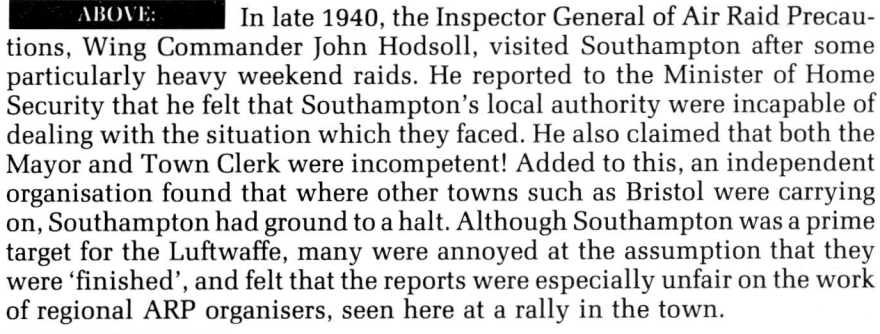

ABOVE: In late 1940, the Inspector General of Air Raid Precautions, Wing Commander John Hodsoll, visited Southampton after some particularly heavy weekend raids. He reported to the Minister of Home Security that he felt that Southampton's local authority were incapable of dealing with the situation which they faced. He also claimed that both the Mayor and Town Clerk were incompetent! Added to this, an independent organisation found that where other towns such as Bristol were carrying on, Southampton had ground to a halt. Although Southampton was a prime target for the Luftwaffe, many were annoyed at the assumption that they were 'finished', and felt that the reports were especially unfair on the work of regional ARP organisers, seen here at a rally in the town.

BOTTOM LEFT: A few days before the announcement of war, evacuation of schoolchildren from the borough was undertaken. Altogether, around 14,000 children were removed to safety. However, a large number were recalled by their parents when the expected early raids did not materialize and it was estimated that half of the children were back in the town when the bombing really did begin. These children seem to be heading further afield than just New Milton, they are embarking on a liner at Southampton Docks, possibly for Canada.

State Lottery,
ALL TO BE DRAWN
8th SEPTEMBER,
WITH
EIGHT EXTRA PRIZES
OF
TICKETS,
Guarranteed to the purchasers of Tickets or Shares at any Office by the Lords of the Treasury.

2 of £16,000	are	£32,000
2 ... 4,000	...	8,000
2 ... 3,000	...	6,000
4 ... 1,000	...	4,000
4 ... 500	...	2,000
6 ... 300	...	1,800
6 ... 200	...	1,200
8 ... 100	...	800
10 ... 50	...	500
10 ... 40	...	400
28 ... 30	...	840
1,990 ... 22	...	42,460
10,000 Tickets		£100,000

Only 5,000 Numbers—two Tickets of each Number, and the drawing of one will decide the other.

EXTRA BENEFITS.
The Four First-drawn Blanks (*not being either of the under-mentioned Numbers*) will each receive a Packet of Twenty Tickets, numbered as follows:
1st drawn Blank . Class A, to have 20 Tickets, No. 1 to No 10 inclusive, in both Classes.
Class B, to have 20 Tickets, 1,751 to 1,760 inclusive, in both Classes.
2d drawn Blank . .Class A, to have 20 Tickets, No 576 to 585 inclusive, in both Classes.
Class B, to have 20 Tickets, No. 2,026 to 2,035 inclusive, in both Classes.
3d drawn Blank . .Class A, to have 20 Tickets, No. 71 to 80 inclusive, in both Classes.
Class B, to have 20 Tickets, No, 3,126 to 3,135 inclusive, in both Classes.
4th drawn Blank . .Class A, to have 20 Tickets, No. 41 to 50 inclusive, in both Classes.
Class B, to have 20 Tickets, No. 4,991 to 5,000 inclusive, in both Classes.

By these EXTRA PRIZES, the Purchaser of a *single* Ticket may realize Thirty, Forty, and even
£50,000.
Shares in Proportion.

TOP LEFT: The interior of the old NAAFI club. This building was situated opposite the Civic Centre, and became known as Marlands Hall. After the NAAFI had finished with it, it was converted into the headquarters of the Southampton Air Training Corps, and a museum dedicated to the memory of Spitfire designer R. J. Mitchell. It was pulled down in April 1985, when the museum and headquarters were transferred to a new building opposite Ocean Village. Now known as The Hall of Aviation, it incorporates the R. J. Mitchell Memorial Museum.

ABOVE: Troops marching down through the town towards the docks in the Second World War. The docks saw massive activity during the conflict. According to the records of the docks manager, on the 17th June 1940, 10,000 troops went through the port. In addition, in the days up to 19th June, 134 steamers plus 85 troop trains used the facilities.

BOTTOM LEFT: An all–too familiar sight during Southampton's blitz. The workman with the wheelbarrow is certainly faced with an uphill task! Enemy aircraft made 57 raids on the town during the war years, and contemporary estimates show that some 475 tons of high explosive bombs were dropped in the area together with over 30,000 incendiary devices.

ABOVE: Palmerston Road *c.,* 1906. The Eagle Public House still trades from the same site overlooking the Park but has a 'mock' Tudor facade these days.

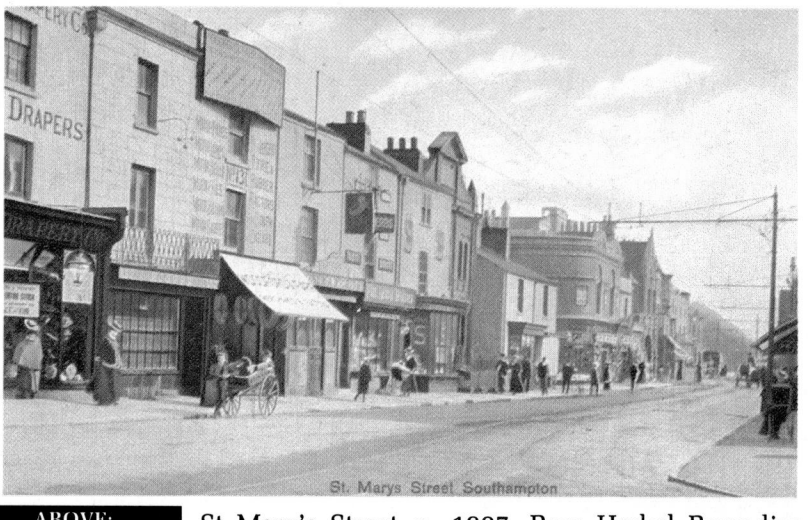

ABOVE: St Mary's Street *c.,* 1907. Pure Herbal Remedies, a pawnbroker, a shoe shop and the Unicorn Pub — an everyday street scene from this period. Further down the street by Deanery Wall a thriving Saturday market operated until well into the evening with 'naptha' flares being used to illuminate the bargains.

ABOVE: Oxford Street *c.,* 1908. A fine early Edwardian view of this favourite haunt for visiting seamen. They would have felt at home here in the London Hotel and other less salubrious pubs and cheap hotels. Most of the shipping offices were located here where many would sign on for their next trip.

ABOVE: Roles Hotel, 37–39 Oxford Street. A promotional card produced possibly by Mr Jakobsson the proprietor, anxious no doubt to get his share of the transient custom from the nearby Terminus Station and the Docks. The reverse of the card also records that 'Trams pass the door to all parts of the Town'.

ABOVE: Docks Post Office, Platform Road, *c.,* 1906. This late Victorian period piece designed by Hawke and built on land purchased from L.S.W.R. did not in fact open until 1905. Certainly its commissioning would have encouraged the North Atlantic and South African mail lines already using the port and may have been instrumental in later arrivals such as the White Star Line. It closed on the 26th April 1967.

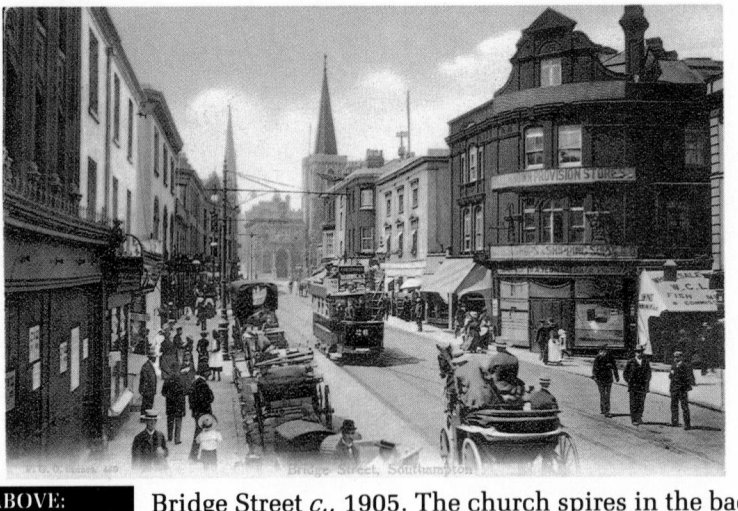

ABOVE: Bridge Street *c.,* 1905. The church spires in the background belong to Holyrood and St Michaels, the fine building inbetween built in 1867 now houses the National Westminster Bank. This thoroughfare is now known as Bernard Street.

ABOVE: Holyrood Church *c.,* 1905. For many years the spiritual heart of the town, this church and six others were lost in the Blitz of 1940−41. The original building of 1320 was rebuilt for the last time in 1849. The remains stand as a formal tribute to merchant seamen lost in the Second World War and an informal reminder of the Blitz years.

ABOVE: East Street *c.,* 1905. A popular shopping area at this time and the first local site for Marks and Spencer, the Yorkshire firm who displayed a large Britannia outside the shop to remind customers they were the original 'Penny Bazaar' ('Don't ask the price, it's a penny'). Percy Hendy also started his business here, originally as bicycle makers then later the country's 'first' Ford car dealer.

TOP LEFT: A total of just over 2,600 high explosive bombs, together with the incendiaries resulted in 630 dead, 898 seriously hurt, and a further 979 slightly injured. Over 900 homes were completely destroyed and a further 2,653 were so seriously damaged that they had to be demolished. It is estimated that 15% of the country's housing stock was destroyed.

ABOVE: In all, over 8,900 properties like the Dymo All Electric Garage in London Road were badly damaged, and another 32,019 slightly damaged. This forced Southampton's rateable value down by 12½% — the third largest drop outside London.

BOTTOM LEFT: This scene from November 1940 shows a home made bomb shelter and a car which has been blown onto the roof by the force of an explosion. Raids continued sporadically for six terrifying months. Even though our fire fighters became efficient at controlling fires once they had begun, by March 1941, very little remained of the High Street or Above Bar, as a result of direct hits from Luftwaffe bombers.

56

ABOVE: This evocative photograph of a living–room rug hanging on the electric tram cables indicates the scale of destruction that was unleashed on the town. It was scenes such as this that residents were often faced with when they emerged from their Anderson shelters as a new day dawned. The exodus from the town was very heavy at night, but most people returned in the morning to their workplaces — if they were still there!

TOP RIGHT: The docks were an obvious target for the Luftwaffe. This devastation is all that remained of the buffet which was situated in number 102 shed. One of the best–remembered raids on the port was when the International Cold Store was hit. It burned out of control for two weeks, fuelled by tons of margarine, rumoured to be an entire weeks' supply for the whole country.

BOTTOM RIGHT: The Southern Railway's docks store did not escape Hitler's Luftwaffe either. This photograph shows the aftermath of the blitz of November and December 1940.

TOP LEFT: The remains of the Peartree Inn in Peartree Road, Woolston. Properties like this one, situated in the vicinity of war effort industries, in this case the Supermarine works, were always under threat.

ABOVE: A solitary tram makes its way along the High Street, while a few citizens trudge through the snow in the winter of 1945. Although the war was at an end, Southampton was faced with a mammoth rebuilding programme to replace the flattened High Street premises many of their cellars can be seen in the middle distance.

BOTTOM LEFT: German POW's arrive at the Town Quay. There was no singing or dancing for them at the Royal Pier. They were captured during the invasion of France in June 1944, and brought back for temporary imprisonment on the Common, before dispersal around the country.

ABOVE:　The Plummer Roddis store at the junction of Above Bar Street was bombed in late 1940. However, the management had the foresight to plan for such an eventuality; various departments were spread out around the town in smaller sites, in much the same way as Spitfire production was to be dispersed around outlying regions. These three views show some of the premises that Plummers pressed into service, one selling millinery, decorative flowers and 'distinctively styled furs'. Another, sandwiched between the Southampton Coal Company and the Christian Science Reading Rooms, concentrating on baby linen and school outfitting. A larger shop provided ladies shoes and electrical appliances on the ground floor, with china, glassware and furnishing sundries above.

TOP LEFT: In the 1960's, several new department stores were planned and built. The earliest of these was Tyrell and Green's in Above Bar, which was designed by Yorke, Rosenberg and Mardell and opened in 1958. This was soon followed by two more multi–storey stores, one of these being Plummers, seen here under construction.

ABOVE: In this photograph, work is already well advanced on Southampton's largest store in Queensway, by builder H. Stevens. Mr Edwin Jones's business became a limited company in 1888. His original premises extended right through East Street to the Park. Edwin Jones at one time ran a flourishing wholesale department that many of the town's retailers used, instead of sending to London for supplies. Edwin Jones himself was Sheriff in 1872, Mayor in 1873 and 1875. He was also a Justice of the Peace and President of the Southampton Polytechnic Institute. In addition to his Manchester House, East Street store, he had another at Queens Buildings, where this new shop is rising. Edwin Jones has since been taken over by the Debenhams group, although many older residents of the town still prefer to call it by the original name.

CHAPTER FIVE

The Centre of Southampton

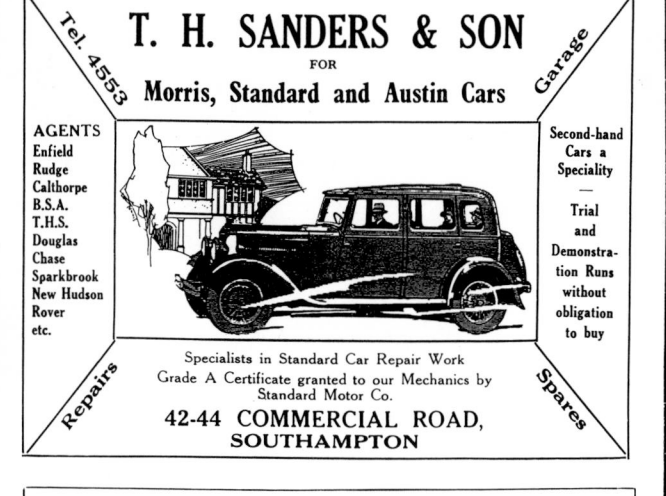

TOP LEFT: Charles Mordaunt, the Earl of Peterborough, developed an existing house into this mansion, and named it Bevois Mount, after the legendary hero of Southampton. The estate lay between the Avenue and Portswood Road. Little remains today, although the house survived until 1940. This photograph dates from *c., 1910.*

TOP RIGHT: Bevois Valley *c., 1915* — originally it had a fine avenue of trees with the river shore on one hand, and the slopes of Bevois Mount on the other. A country road wound up the hill until it was lost in the shadows of the Portswood trees, there had already been a good deal of development when this photograph was taken!

BOTTOM LEFT: Six Dials, looking West *c., 1910.* So named because of the half dozen roads that once led off this junction. This photograph was taken from the end of Northam Road, where a mecca for antique hunters has sprung up to lend the area some of its previous vitality.

Six Dials looking East, Southampton.

THE JUNCTION — SOUTHAMPTON AP. 25. 1908.

TOP LEFT: Six Dials looking East *c.,* 1910. On the left is St Mary's Road, and the district office of the Royal Liver Friendly Society, and on the right St Mary's Street where Kingsland Market can be found; even today a favourite haunt for Southampton's bargain hunters.

ABOVE: Tram Junction in a heavy snowstorm on April 25th 1908. Plummers store can be seen on the corner, through the blizzard. This store still exists, albeit in a new, post–war building.

BOTTOM LEFT: The Junction at Prospect Place *c.,* 1938 — this time in more favourable weather conditions. The small building in the centre of the scene with the pitched roof became an information kiosk. This photograph is taken a few yards past the site of Tyrell and Green's current store.

JUNCTION, PROSPECT PLACE, SOUTHAMPTON.

Lieut. **SHACKLETON**
Will give his Illustrated Lecture on
'**Nearest the South Pole**'
In the
HARTLEY HALL, SOUTHAMPTON,
TUESDAY, Nov. 2nd, at 8.0.
The Chair will be taken by
Principal RICHARDS, D.Sc., M.A.
RESERVED SEATS, 5/- 3/6 UNRESERVED, 2/- 1/-
Doors open at 7.30. Carriages at 10.
Plan may be seen and seats booked at Messrs. Godfrey & Co., Ltd., 87, Above Bar, Southampton.
Kinematograph Pictures.

1 SOUTHAMPTON. — General View. — LL.

CM.5002. SOUTHAMPTON CIVIC CENTRE.

AERIAL VIEW, SOUTHAMPTON, DOCKS STATION & S.W. HOTEL. (4319)

TOP LEFT: This rather misty view was obtained from the London and South Western Railway Hotel in Canute Road. This large building houses both BBC local radio and television studios, together with the offices of Cunard. It is now known as South Western House, the BBC are soon to desert this fine old building for a modern purpose built facility close to the Civic Centre.

ABOVE: An aerial view showing the Civic Centre to good effect. The foundation stone for this building (designed by Berry Webbers and sponsored by Sir Sydney Kimber) was laid by the Duke of York, on the 1st of July 1930. The total cost of the completed Centre has been calculated at £750,000. The bells in the clock tower (sometimes referred to as Kimber's Chimney) play 'Our God Our Help In Ages Past' in recognition of the composer Isaac Watts. This picture dates from after 1940 as the last portion, the Arts Block has now been completed albeit fairly recently.

BOTTOM LEFT: This aerial view highlights the sheer size and grandeur of the South Western Hotel which stands out clearly in the centre of the photograph. The hotel was not completed until 1872, probably the finest Victorian building in Southampton it was constructed in an elaborate French Renaissance style. The railway terminus at the rear (Terminus Station) was designed by William Tite in Italianate style and was opened in 1840.

COSSER. PHOTO; SOUTHAMPTON.

Children's Gala, The Baths, Southampton.

TOP LEFT: An unusual view of West Station, this time seen from the River Test. The whole of this area was reclaimed, and the new docks built out into the river, leaving the Western Esplanade some distance from the water. (See also Page 17, top right).

ABOVE: The Southampton Public Baths (*c.,* 1904) were situated on the Western shore, and opened in March 1892. The building had a frontage of 224 feet, with the principal entrance being flanked with two towers. Inside were two covered swimming baths and forty slipper baths, supplied with both salt and fresh water. Also available was a suite of Turkish baths. At the rear was a further open air pool of half an acre, as seen in this photograph. The total cost of the establishment was about £18,000. This view shows a Children's Gala with what appears to be a pipe band on the platform. (see also Page 17, bottom left).

BOTTOM LEFT: Another bathing scene, this time from the late 1930's, when the Lido was popular. The Marlands shopping development is now being constructed in its wake. Today's modern answer to the Public Baths and the Lido is Centre 2000 a complete 'Leisure' complex situated just a few hundred yards and some 50 years away from this scene.

BARGATE, SOUTHAMPTON. (13)

219133.J.V.

F. G. O. Stuart, 1930

The Bargate, Southampton

TOP LEFT: Bargate as seen from the High Street *c.,* 1929. In this photograph, cars have taken the place of horses, carriages and carts. After considerable debate, the Estates Committee of the Council finally commissioned a scheme in 1928 to construct roadways around the outside of the Bargate to assist traffic flow.

BOTTOM LEFT: The Bargate from Above Bar Street, prior to 1932 when leases on properties adjoining the monument were acquired and work began on the eastern bypass. The western part of the Bargate Circus, however, was not started until 1938.

ABOVE: This photograph shows trams running over the new tracks on the eastern part of the Bargate Circus. This brought to an end two hundred years of complaints from various vested interests about the obstruction, which at one point threatened to result in the demolition of the Bargate altogether.

LAYOUT AT THE BARGATE :-

15 JAN 00 TO 23 APL 32

24 APL 32 TO 4 JNE 38

5 JNE 38 TO 31 DEC 49

UNTIL 1939

The Old Walls, Southampton

TOP LEFT: Southampton's West Gate at the turn of the century. It was outside this gateway that, on the morning of Sunday 4th October 1338, a motley gang of French and Genoese pirates landed and laid waste to the prosperous merchant's quarter of the town taking with them, amongst other things the King's wine stocks. It was through this gate that Henry V marched his troops on their way to Agincourt in 1415. It was said that the circular saw was invented in the house on the extreme right by Walter Taylor (1734–1803).

ABOVE: The Old Walls *c.,* 1950. Here Western Esplanade by name alone suggests its original position on Southampton waterfront, land reclamation being the reason for its apparent movement!

BOTTOM LEFT: Tudor House was built as a town house for a gentleman called Sir John Dawtrey in about 1500. It was constructed on, and incorporated into it several earlier properties. It is undoubtedly one of the finest late medieval houses in the country. The house has been extensively restored and is open to the public as one of the City's museums.

Tudor House, Southampton

High Street, Southampton

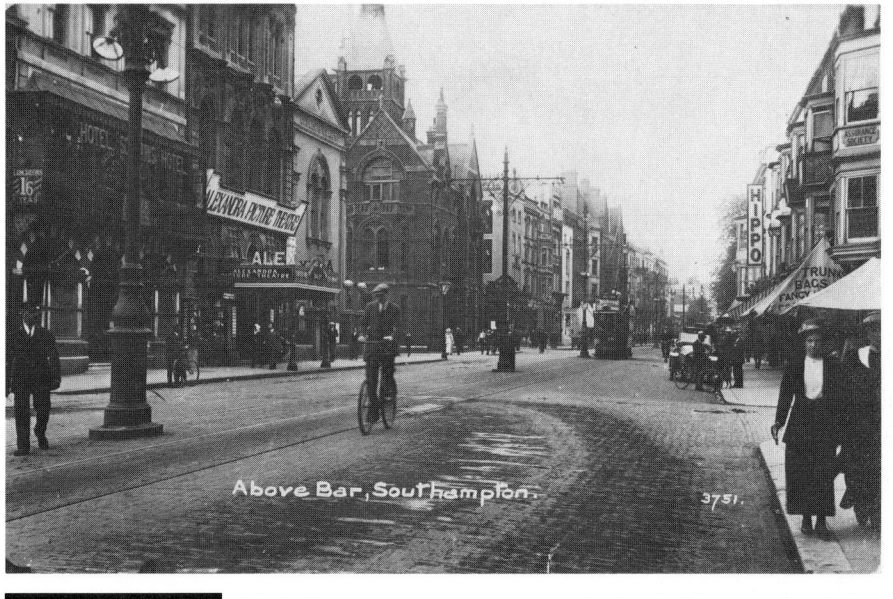

Above Bar, Southampton. 3751.

TOP LEFT: High Street *c.,* 1926. Note the Dolphin Hotel, one of the oldest surviving properties in the area. The distinctive bow windows, however, are a recent addition. At one time it was a coaching inn often visited by Royalty, and many other renowned personalities of the early 19th Century, including Jane Austen. There has been an Inn on this site since 1432.

ABOVE: Sadly, very few architectural features of Southampton's Above Bar Street survive today — Hitler's bombs made sure of that. This photograph of 1919 shows how the town looked at the end of the Great War. In 1931, a traffic census recorded that 4,500 cars used the thoroughfare during the year, they were outnumbered by bicycles which tallied 10,000!

BOTTOM LEFT: The High Street from Holyrood dating from the late 1940's. The effects of the wartime blitz are very evident on the left–hand side of the road. One would have expected the humble horse and cart to have disappeared from the streets by this time but a horse drawn vehicle can be seen, possibly a coalman's cart, visible on the right of the picture outside the Dolphin Hotel.

LONDON ROAD, SOUTHAMPTON.

Ordnance Office, Southampton.

TOP LEFT: The Oxford public house in St Mary's Road undergoing some painting and decorating work (*c.,* 1910). This quartet of white coated painters are putting the finishing touches to their handiwork; alas 'Barlows Celebrated Ales' are no longer available from this pub which still stands but no doubt serves 'keg' beer in its stead.

ABOVE: London Road *c.,* 1910. This area included many fine buildings in the early days of the century. The imposing Victorian, Central Library and Art Gallery were built here in 1892 at a cost of £6,500. The facilities were later transferred to the new Civic Centre, where they have remained ever since. The Church on the right of the scene is St Paul's, which is no longer standing.

BOTTOM LEFT: Ordnance Office, London Road. Established locally in 1841 the Survey had been forced to quit the Map Office in the Tower of London after a fire. Sixty years later, they employed around 700 local people. These offices in London Road were badly damaged in the 1940 blitz and once again the Survey was on the move, this time to the Crabwood site where their new modern facility was opened in 1964.

TOP LEFT: This shows the Grand Theatre which stood opposite West Marlands, next to the old Hants and Dorset Omnibus Company headquarters. It was first opened in 1898, and survived until 1964 when it was finally demolished to make way for a development of shops and offices.

ABOVE: This area was, for many years, known as 'The Ditches', although it is correctly termed Lower Canal Walk. Until the blitz, this road was visited by considerable numbers of shoppers keen on hunting out a bargain on a Saturday afternoon.

BOTTOM LEFT: Lower Canal Walk *c.,* 1913. This busy thoroughfare was nothing more than a simple, narrow alleyway with tiny lock–up shops that sold almost anything you could think of. Most of the proprietors kept their doors open until midnight. This photograph shows a butcher's shop of that time.

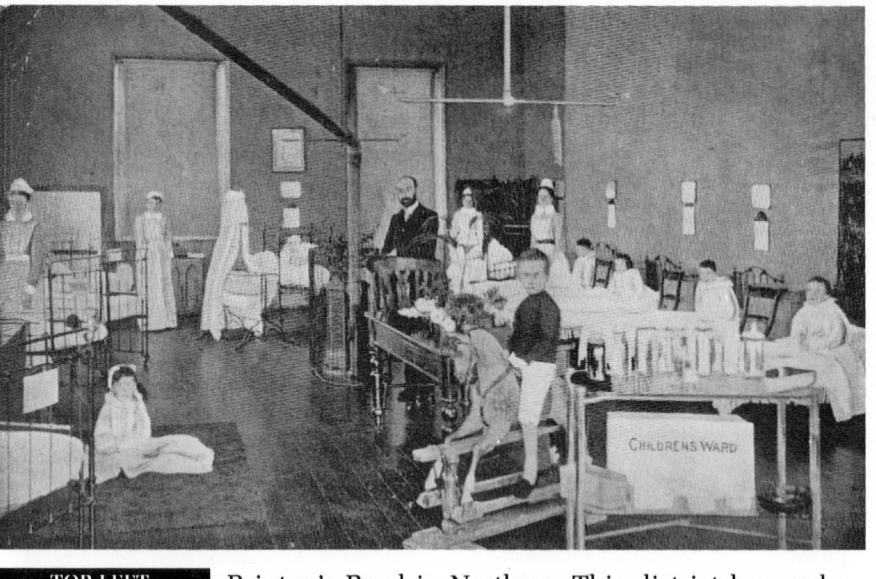

TOP LEFT: Brinton's Road in Northam. This district has undergone almost complete change, very little remains of the true old Northam today, apart that is from a few ancient cottages dotted about, a pub or two and the gasworks.

BOTTOM LEFT: Not the blitz, but devastation caused by a gas explosion at the Southampton Conservative Club in Oak Road, Northam on Monday May 1st 1905. The blast was caused by a defective gas main, which wrecked the billiard room, leaving two people seriously injured.

ABOVE: The Children's Ward of the Royal South Hants and Southampton Hospital in Fanshawe Street. In 1923, the income arising from investments, subscriptions and donations was about £20,000 per year.

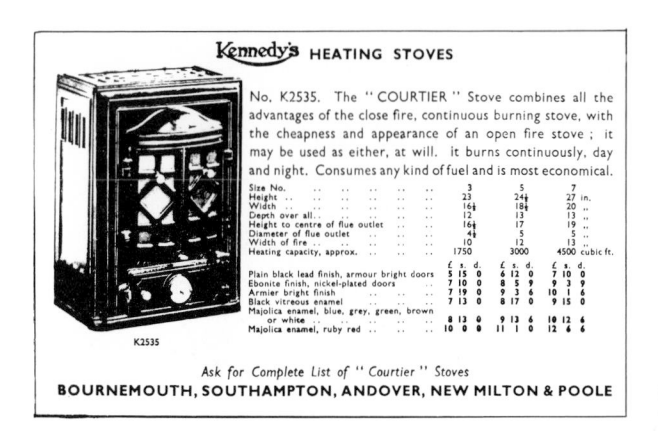

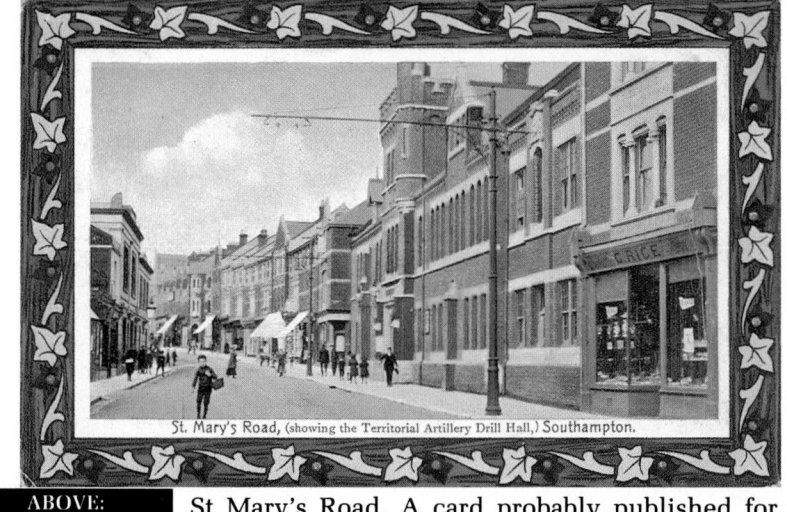

ABOVE: New Polygon Hotel, 1937. The original Polygon built in 1768 was part of a grand scheme to rival Bath with an Assembly Room and handsome grounds to attract the 'Spa' visitor, the plan floundered in 1773, the last 'season' being celebrated a year later. The new hotel was completed to an Adamson design, building by Dukes of Southampton, in 1937. It is arguably one of the better examples of Odeon design and the current proprietors have plans to restore it as such.

ABOVE: St Mary's Road. A card probably published for the Christmas market at the turn of the century showing the Territorial Artillery Drill Hall. Together with Onslow Road these two thoroughfares were home to many thriving small businesses. The St Mary's Sports Centre now occupies the Drill Hall site.

ABOVE: Royal South Hants Hospital c., 1907. This fine 'italinate' building in Fanshawe Street was originally completed in 1838 and housed 130 beds, new wings were added in 1900 and opened by Princess Henry of Battenberg.

ABOVE: East Gate, c., 1908. One of the two eastern entrances to the walled town. This gate was also known as York Gate and was built in 1769. Sadly it did not survive the redevelopment plan intended to repair the last remnants of Blitz damage and was demolished in 1961.

ABOVE: God's House Gate *c.,* 1909. The original eastern entrance to the town and together with the Tower, the key to the defensive walls that were constructed to encircle the town (and castle) in the early 15th century. The town gaol was still housed in this tower until 1855 when it became a grain warehouse. The Platform Tavern is signed on the right of the picture.

ABOVE: The Wool House, Bugle Street, *c.,* 1905. Built by Beaulieu's monastic order around 1375, it contained the town's weigh—beam on which all wool coming through the port had to be weighed. Its subsequent uses have been many including a place in aviation history when E. R. Moon built an early aircraft here in 1910. It has been superbly restored and now houses the City's Maritime Museum.

ABOVE: Cobden Bridge *c.,* 1906. A tram is about to leave the Bitterne Park side to cross the first Cobden bridge. The Phoenix boatyard in the right foreground was to grow considerably over the next 30 years.

ABOVE: Floating Bridge *c.,* 1908. At this time bridges Nos. 7, 8 and 9 were operating. Steam driven, they had been constructed in 1892, 1896 and 1900. No. 7 was sunk in a collision with the steam tug *Fawley* in March 1928. It was raised, but eventually scrapped in 1940. The two masted ships would have been unloading coal or timber. The large shape of Westlakes corn store at American Wharf can be seen on the extreme left.

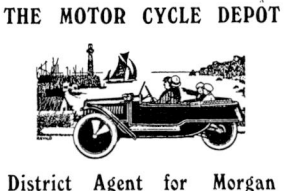

TOP LEFT: This photograph, taken in 1912 at Stag Gates, shows how work is progressing on track laying for the tramway service out to Portswood. The laying of these lines caused considerable upheaval, and it was perhaps fortunate that the roads in those days carried much less motor traffic.

ABOVE: Western Esplanade on December 26th 1912. This shows Weymouth Terrace flooded out at high tide. This terrace is no more, having been demolished to make way for recent re–development schemes.

BOTTOM LEFT: This view dates from 1880, and was taken from the top of Forty Steps in the Old Walls. These steps were built to serve a roadway that had been constructed from the Long Rooms to the station in around 1835. The tower on the right is said to date from the 14th century, and at one time formed the north western defence of the town.

TOP LEFT: A photograph from the late 1950's, when steam trains still ran through Southampton's Central Station. A considerable amount of building work is going on at the Civic Centre.

ABOVE: Royal patronage stimulated Southampton in the mid 18th century. The three younger brothers of King George III — the Dukes of York, Gloucester and Cumberland — became regular visitors to the town during the heyday of its Spa period. This photograph shows Cumberland Place in 1880.

BOTTOM LEFT: The demolition of King's Cinema in St Mary Street. The Plume of Feathers public house still trades from the same spot. Near here can be found Kingsland Street Market which survives today, and has recently been given its own purpose—built roof.

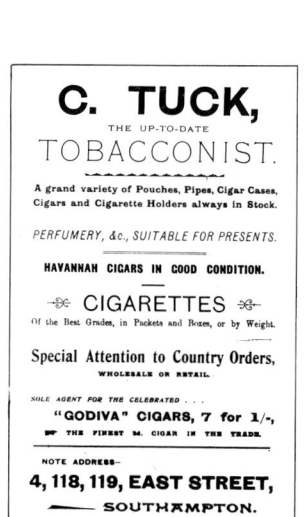

TOP LEFT: Hillier's one of Southampton's earliest record shops situated at 76 Northam Road. Records are advertised at just 3d, and we are in luck, gramophone main springs are back in stock. There is also a large array of musical instruments inside the shop, and even an offer of music lessons.

BOTTOM LEFT: Still with the same area, on the junction of Northam and St Marks Roads was W. G. Searle's tobacconist and stationers. This photograph was taken in about 1920. The proud owners are standing in the doorway. This is now an antique jewellery shop.

ABOVE: Summers and Payne, chandlers and engineers who had a yard and works at Belvidere and Northam; with an office and shop at 85 High Street.

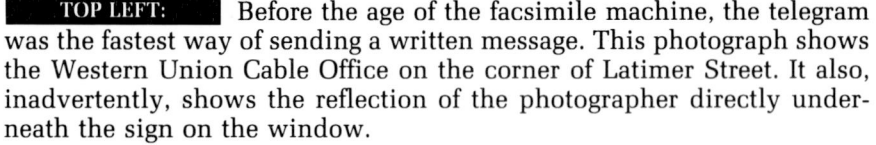

TOP LEFT: Before the age of the facsimile machine, the telegram was the fastest way of sending a written message. This photograph shows the Western Union Cable Office on the corner of Latimer Street. It also, inadvertently, shows the reflection of the photographer directly underneath the sign on the window.

BOTTOM LEFT: The High Street offices of the Liverpool and London and Globe Insurance Company, this part of the building was known as Guildhall Chambers. The property at number one is about to close according to the bills stuck to the windows, which also indicate that the original firm F. J. Trippe (a gentleman's tailor) is to relocate to Bedford Place.

ABOVE: Southampton's Central Hall, built on the corner of St Mary's Street and Marsh Lane. This was taken in the days before a busy dual carriageway passed its doors. Notice also, the advert for a BBC concert.

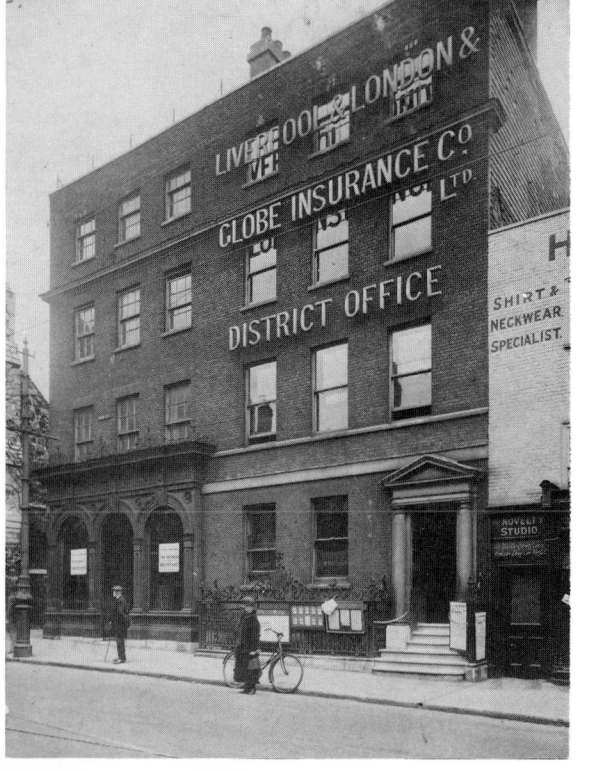

TOP LEFT: A view from Hoglands Park across to Queens Buildings, which is now the site of Debenhams Department Store. This area used to be known as the Strand and Canal Walk. Notice the carriage waiting under the trees. This was a Christmas greeting posted at 10pm on 24th December 1905.

BOTTOM LEFT: The offices of Royal Mail Lines Ltd. The sign tells us that Pacific Steam Navigation Company offered passenger and freight services to South America, the West Indies and the North Pacific coast. This road housed many of the shipping lines, and the Union Castle offices can be seen in the background at the left of the photograph.

78

ABOVE: On the 12th September 1809, the Maquis of Landsdowne presented a statue of King George III to the town. This was placed in the niche on the south face of the Bargate, replacing the statue of Queen Anne which had been there since 1705. Queen Anne's statue was moved to a new position within the building, where she remains today.

BOTTOM LEFT: The Bargate in 1914, featuring Pembroke Square. Notice the posters affixed to the railings asking the local citizens to enlist 'for all branches of His Majesty's Army'. There were three local recruiting offices, one in the town and at 31 Portswood and at 310 Shirley Road. Pembroke Square was demolished to make way for the Bargate Circus Road.

CHAPTER SIX

Bridges, Floating and Otherwise

SOUTHAMPTON & ITCHEN

FLOATING BRIDGE & ROADS Co.

No. *218* **SEASON TICKET.**

It is Certified that Mr. *C. H. Le Marchel*

is entitled to Pass Free by the Bridges of the Company

as a Foot Passenger (subject to the conditions on the back

hereof) from *Jan* 1896 to *Dec 31 –* 1896

W Cross _____ Collector.

Signature of Holder _____

[SEE OVER

NOTICE.

To servants of the Southampton and Itchen Bridge Company.

No servant of the Company whilst on duty on either of the Bridges is allowed to leave the Bridge for the purpose of procuring any intoxicating drink.

If detected in so doing he will be fined One Shilling, and if this does not stop the offence, he will be dismissed.

The Toll Collectors are instructed to inform the Manager through Mr. Cross, if they see men on duty pass through the Toll Gates for this purpose.

Any case of intoxication, if well authenticated, will be followed by dismissal.

W. G. LANKESTER,
MANAGER.

April 17th, 1880.

ALFRED RANDLE, Machine Printer, 161, High Street, Southampton.

SOUTHAMPTON & ITCHEN

FLOATING BRIDGE & ROADS COMPANY.

REGULATIONS FOR BOATMEN.

1. The Boatmen are required to have their Boats ready to receive Passengers at Five o'clock every morning, and the Boats will continue to work till half-past Twelve at night, except on Sundays, when they will cease to run at midnight.

2. Whenever required the Boatmen are to work the boats at any other times during the night, for which special service each Boatman will be paid extra wages.

3. The Boatmen are expressly prohibited from taking or demanding any Toll or money whatsoever from passengers, except after Toll hours.

4. The Boatmen are required to row their own boats, and under no circumstances to allow more than one oar to be rowed by a passenger.

5. No Boatman is permitted to leave the service of the Company without giving one week's notice on receiving his wages on Saturday.

6. The Boatmen are expressly prohibited from leaving their Boats during the time they are on duty, and the violation of this rule will render them liable to dismissal without notice.

7. Should any property be discovered in the Boats the Boatman shall immediately deliver the same to the nearest Toll Keeper to be taken care of until claimed and identified by the owner.

In case of any misconduct or instance of insobriety of a Boatman, or any insult or incivility to passengers, or any violation of the rules of the Company, the Managing Director is empowered to discharge such offender without any notice, and all accruing wages will be forfeited to the Company.

By order of the Directors,

F. BERESFORD TURNER,
Clerk.

Southampton, 10th June, 1874.

A. RANDLE, Printing Offices, High St., Southampton.

DAY, SUMMERS & C°.
Engineers & Shipbuilders.
SOUTHAMPTON.
1896.

Makers' Plate — Bridge No. 8

MORDEY, CARNEY
(SOUTHAMPTON) LTD.
Engineers & Shipbuilders
SOUTHAMPTON
1900

Makers' Plate — Bridge No. 9

DAY, SUMMERS & C° L°.
Engineers & Shipbuilders,
SOUTHAMPTON
N°193.   1928

Makers' Plate — Bridge No. 10

DESIGNED BY
CHARLES W. MURRAY.
M.I.Mar.E.,M.I.N.E.,
Consulting Engineer & Naval Architect
SOUTHAMPTON.

Southampton and Itchen
FLOATING BRIDGE & ROAD COMPANY.

NOTICE !

ON THURSDAY MORNING, April 20th,
the Bridge WILL BE STOPPED for a few
hours after 6 o'clock, a.m. for the purpose of
repairing the Chain.

W. G. LANKESTER, *Manager.*

April 19th, 1876.

A. RANDLE, Printing Works, 139 and 140, High Street, Southampton.

TOLL ON DOGS

One HALFPENNY each
DURING
ORDINARY BRIDGE HOURS.

A. RANDLE, Printer, Southampton.

Bitterne Park from Cobden Bridge.

TOP LEFT: Northam Bridge *c.,* 1850 was constructed of timber in the 1790's. It made the east bank of the river a popular place to live, and resulted in a number of fine houses, such as Ridgeway Castle, Peartree and Chessel being built. Before the bridge was built, traffic could only cross this formidable natural barrier at Mans Bridge. The Corporation took over the bridge in March 1929, and shortly afterwards abolished the tolls. Originally there had been charges for animals, carts and wagons, but not people.

ABOVE: When first built, Cobden Bridge became the scene of pitched battles between the 'local lads' of St Deny's, and those from across the water at Bitterne. The antagonism was due to what the Bitternites perceived as an unwelcome invasion by 'townies' into their country area on highdays and holidays. The tribal warfare between them was eventually curbed by a police baton charge one Sunday afternoon in 1885, sometimes referred to as 'The Battle of Cobden Bridge'.

BOTTOM LEFT: This photograph, taken from Cobden Bridge, shows Bitterne Triangle before the clock tower arrived — the tower that now dominates the scene originally stood in Above Bar. This scene dates from around 1914. The tramway across the river was inaugurated in 1902. In 1923, the service was extended to nearby Bullar Road.

Cobden Bridge, Bitterne Park.

Floating Bridge, Southampton.

ABOVE: Cobden Bridge was built in 1883 by the National Land Company who had purchased a considerable amount of land at Bitterne Park for housing development, they gave the bridge to the town, presumably to avoid its upkeep costs. This photograph however dates from about 1949. (See also Page 72).

TOP RIGHT: Northam Bridge. After the timber bridge came an iron one, then finally this new concrete structure completed in 1954. The photograph shows the unfinished bridge designed to take the considerable increase in traffic flow. A situation brought about largely from the increased use of private motor vehicles.

BOTTOM RIGHT: A scene from 1933. The first floating bridge was built near Devonport and first operated on the 23rd of November 1836. A new iron vessel was subsequently built in 1854 by Joseph Hodgkinson of Crosshouse Foundry. It cost £12,870 and lasted for 42 years. Later bridges were built by the Northam yard of Day Summers and these steam powered vessels (operated by Southampton Corporation from 1934) did sterling work until replaced by the first of two new, diesel—powered versions, delivered by Thornycrofts in 1962 and 1964.

CITY OF SOUTHAMPTON TRANSPORT DEPARTMENT
FLOATING BRIDGE TOLLS
SINGLE FARES

SOLO MOTOR CYCLE, SCOOTER, AUTO-CYCLE OR HAND TRUCK	7P
TRI-CAR, THREE WHEEL CAR, OR MOTOR CYCLE COMBINATION	12P
ALL FOUR WHEELED CARS, AND COMMERCIAL VEHICLES UP TO 16ft LONG	16P
ALL COMMERCIAL VEHICLES OVER 16ft LONG AND UP TO 5 TONS (LIMIT)	35P
MOTOR COACHES NOT EXCEEDING 4 TONS 10 CWT.	35P
VEHICLES DRAWING CARAVANS, TRAILERS, OR BOATS	35P
VEHICLES DRIVEN BY REGISTERED DISABLED DRIVERS CARRYING ROAD FUND EXEMPTION DISC	FREE
FOOT PASSENGERS, DRIVERS, CYCLES, AND PRAMS	FREE

ABOVE: Itchen Floating Bridge. This priceless piece of nostalgia was rescued from the hulk of the last bridge (No. 14) before it was sold off. These fares seem quite competitive compared with today's road bridge tolls, certainly foot passengers seem to have done badly out of the affair, it may still be free but now they have to walk!

TOP RIGHT: Itchen Bridge. A bridge here had been originally planned as far back as 1920, the proposal was put forward again in 1936 and 1947. However, it was deferred in view of work needing to be done on Northam Bridge. A Bill was eventually prepared for Parliament in 1960 for a bridge with a centre span of not less than 350 feet and a clearance of 80 feet at high water to allow the passage of ships up the river. The scheme looked set to go ahead until the Ministry of Transport decided that it was unnecessary and refused to provide funding for three quarters of the cost. They argued that the south coast trunk route later to become the M27, provided the necessary access.

BOTTOM RIGHT: The permanent bridge was built after the Council agreed to a tender of £5,710,630 from Kier Ltd., at a meeting on February 13th 1973. It eventually opened on Wednesday 1st June 1977. Ten days later, the floating bridges ran for the very last time, signalling the end of a 140 year tradition. This ticket was one of the last issued. It carries the initial letters of the Southampton & Itchen Bridge Co.

SOUTHAMPTON AND ITCHEN FLOATING BRIDGE AND ROADS COMPANY.

WHEREAS it has been found that in the rush which was made by the men crossing by the Workmen's Trip from Woolston last evening that 195 Tickets were wrongfully retained, and have not since been returned.

NOTICE IS HEREBY GIVEN, that unless the aforesaid Tickets are returned to the Company's Collector, at the Woolston Toll House, before Ten o'clock a.m. on Saturday, the 15th instant, that the Directors have resolved to discontinue the Half Toll privilege hitherto granted to Workmen, and that on and after Monday, the 17th instant, the FULL TOLL of One Penny will be henceforth charged.

By Order of the Directors,

F. BERESFORD TURNER,
Clerk.

Wednesday, 12th September, 1883.

Hampshire Advertiser Company, Limited : Printed by Henry King, 38, High Street, Southampton.

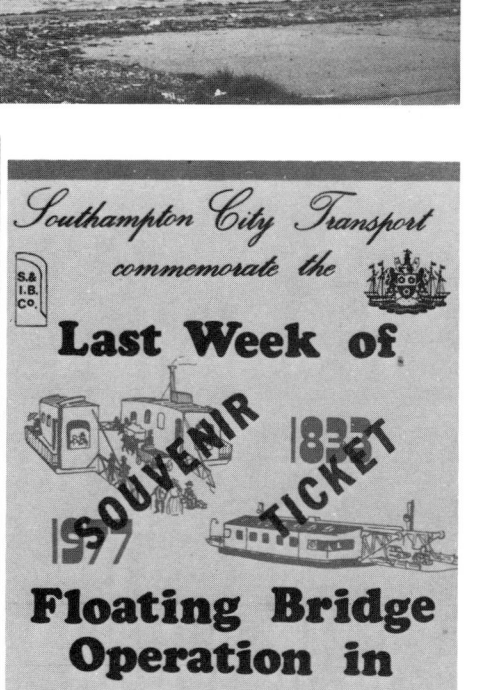

Southampton City Transport
commemorate the

Last Week of

SOUVENIR

1977   1833

TICKET

Floating Bridge Operation in Southampton

10p	Ticket No: 3331	W.S. Lewis B.A., M.C.I.T Southampton City Transport 226, Portswood Road Southampton SO9 4XS

CHAPTER SEVEN

Advertisements, announcements, trade cards and assorted printed ephemera

The earliest known form of advertisement dates from around 3000 years ago. It was discovered by an archaeologist in the ruins of Thebes. It offered a gold coin in return for a runaway slave. During the Middle Ages, the spoken word was the principal form of recommendation, and there was nothing that could really be termed advertising apart perhaps from signs outside shops and 'guild' membership badges. However, the invention of movable type in about 1450, by Johannes Gutenberg, made it possible to produce mutiple copies of books, periodicals and broadsheets very cheaply. This soon ushered in the age of advertising.

By the start of this century, the printed media had become very well established, and all the Southampton—based publications carried adverts, a considerable number of these are included within this final section, I am certain that you will be amazed at the prices of some items.

What I noticed from the following was a marked lack of 'hype', and what appears to be a much more genuine concern for the satisfaction of the customer. Although examples of 'knocking copy' can be found it is a very rare occurrence. I enjoyed looking at these somehow more cultured, commercial campaigns. Some readers may even have their memories jogged by some of the local trade names and products and the family businesses now long since closed down or absorbed by rapacious chains of multiple retailers.

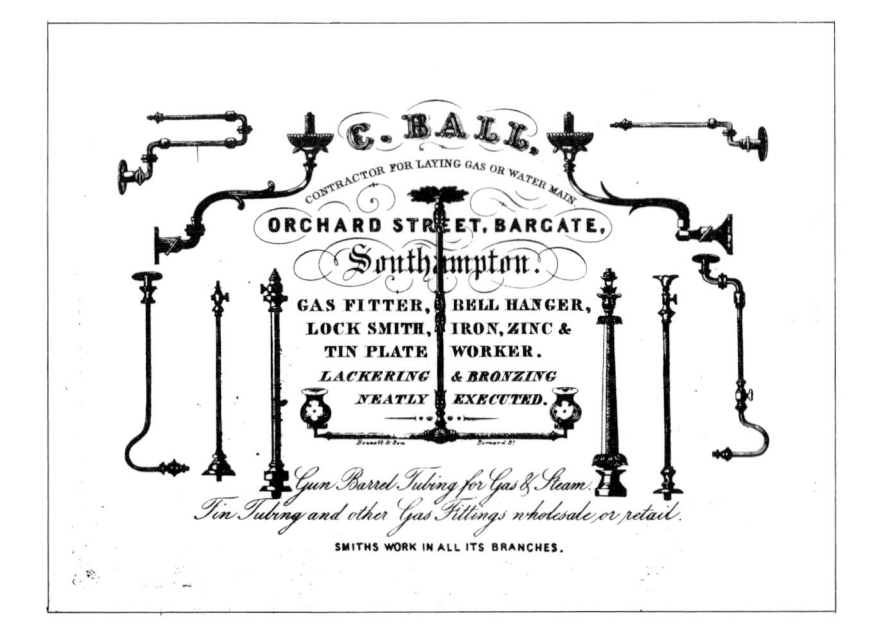

WHOLESALE & FOR EXPORTATION

165

UMBRELLAS
PARASOLS
GLOVES
BRACES
STOCKS
CAPS
SILK
BEAVER
WATERPROOF
HATS
MACKINTOSH
PILLOWS
COATS
CAPES

ELLYETT 165

CAZE
TAKER 164

DRESS AND FROCK COATS
Of superior cloth made to measure.
TROUSERS AND WAISTCOATS, of the Newest Patterns.
PALETOTS & OUTSIDE WRAPPERS
In great variety.
SUITS OF UNIFORM AND OF LIVERY.
Yachting, Linen and Long Cloth Shirts at the Lowest Prices,
PORTMANTEAUS,
CARPET BAGS, HAT CASES.

AGENT
For WATERPROOF PARAMA COATS, CAPES, LEGGINGS,
OVERSHOES,
SWIMMING BELTS, AYCKBOURN'S FLOATS, AND
LIFE JACKETS OF EVERY DESCRIPTION.

SOUTHAMPTON, 165, HIGH STREET.

Purchased at the **HAT, CAP, AND OUTFITTING WAREHOUSE** of
RICHARD D. ELLYETT,

BY

LONDON HOUSE.
S. S. IRELAND,
Furnishing Upholsterer, Cabinet Maker,
JOINER, &c.
East Street, corner of Richard Lane,
SOUTHAMPTON.
PAPER HANGING   FUNERALS PERFORMED

LADIES' NEEDLE WORK MOUNTED.

PLACE

BENNETT
Engraver
& PRINTER,
&c.
ABOVE BAR
SOUTHAMPTON

ENGRAVING AND ENAMELING ON IVORY.

BY SPECIAL   APPOINTMENT

WILLIAM STORROR,
UPHOLSTERER & CABINET MAKER
To the Queen.
APPRAISER, PAPER HANGER & UNDERTAKER,
58 & 59 French Street, Southampton.

Totton, near Southampton.
To be SOLD by AUCTION,
AT THE
ANCHOR INN, ELING,
BY Mr. DELL,
On THURSDAY, AUGUST 17, 1820, between the hours of 4 and 6 o'clock in the afternoon,
IN FIVE LOTS,
(Agreeably to CONDITIONS as will be produced at the time of Sale)
ALL THAT
VALUABLE LEASEHOLD
Property
SITUATED AT
TOTTON, NETLEY, and *TESTWOOD.*

LOT I.—All that neat and well-built COTTAGE and TENE-
MENT, situated in the Village of TOTTON, with a large Garden, Yard, Stable; Cart, Wood, and
Turf Houses; 5 Acres of arable and 3 Acres of rich meadow Land.   443

LOT II.—Three ACRES of arable LAND, at the back of
Mr. HAYTER's, butcher. This land is well adapted for building on, the situation is healthy
and pleasant, commands pleasing and extensive views of land and water.   175

LOT III.—Four ACRES of COPPICE LAND, at NETLEY,
near CARMER.   25

LOT IV.—Four DITTO, at TESTWOOD.   12

LOT V.—The run for a Horse in the Salt-Marsh.   46
                                                                     £ 697

The above Property is held under Christi College, in the University of Oxford, for three lives, 15, 24, 30, and a
widowhood. Possession may be had immediately. Further particulars may be had of the Auctioneer, at his office, No. 11,
Hanover Buildings, Southampton; or Mr. TILLER, at Eling, who will shew the premises.

PRINTED BY E. SKELTON & CO. SOUTHAMPTON.

ROYAL YORK HOTEL, SOUTHAMPTON.

ROYAL YORK HOTEL.

George Quick begs most respectfully to announce to the Nobility Gentry & Public in general that this Hotel has been entirely rebuilt and extensively enlarged, and the utmost care taken in the arrangement thereof to render it conducive to the comfort and convenience of those who may be pleased to honor the Establishment with their support.

Excellent Stabling & Lock up Coach Houses.—Post Horses, Chaises &c. GENUINE WINES.

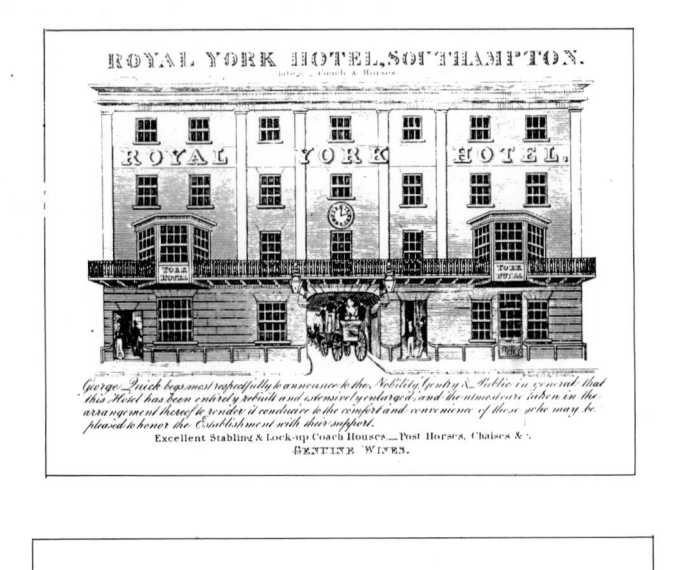

D. PURKIS,
Ship Builder, &c.
SOUTHAMPTON.
FLOATING DRY DOCK
For Ships 600 tons O.M.

BY SPECIAL APPOINTMENT
ANDREWS,
Coach Builder to Her Majesty
11, Above Bar,—Opposite the Coach & Horses Inn,
SOUTHAMPTON.
Carriages built to order on the most approved principles on moderate terms & carefully packed for Exportation.

20, High St. Southampton.
JAS. TRIGGS,
Cabinet Maker, Upholsterer,
UNDERTAKER, AUCTIONEER,
& Appraiser.

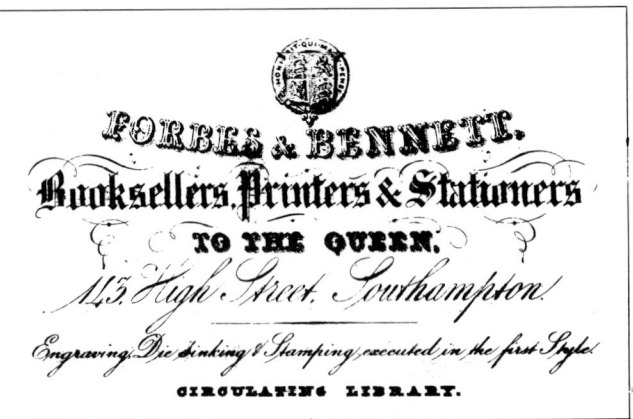

FORBES & BENNETT,
Booksellers, Printers & Stationers
TO THE QUEEN,
115, High Street, Southampton.
Engraving, Die Sinking & Stamping, executed in the first Style
CIRCULATING LIBRARY.

VISITING & ADDRESS CARDS.
BILL HEADS, BOOK PLATES, LABELS &c.
H.W. CROPP,
Engraver
and Copper Plate Printer
111, High Street,
SOUTHAMPTON.
Door Plates and Office Seals.
Printing in Gold Silver &c.
Arms, Crests, Initials & Inscriptions on Silver, Ivory, Pearl, &c.